11 DEC 2017

MANCHESTER
CITY COUNCIL

28 DEC 2017

27 JAN 2018

17 FEB 2018

22 AUG 2020

Please return / renew this item
by the last date shown.
Books may also be renewed by
phone or the Internet.

Tel: 0161 254 7777

www.manchester.gov.uk/libraries

Jean-François Mallet

SIMPLISSIME

LIGHT

THE EASIEST

COOKBOOK

IN THE

WORLD

**Light recipes to read at a glance
and make in a flash**

hamlyn

This is not a diet cookbook but rather a collection of light (or lighter) recipes that are healthy, tasty and varied. It comes in response to a question I am regularly asked by my friends, both girls and boys: how to live on ordinary everyday food without putting on weight and only eating three lettuce leaves, a yoghurt and an apple.

It is possible to enjoy your food while keeping an eye on your figure and your health, come up with new dishes that provide five fruits and vegetables a day and only use a few ingredients you have in your refrigerator or your larder, or are easy to find in the corner shop.

In my second book, I want to share everyday recipes with you that are quick and easy and will suit all tastes. Combining simple flavours and ingredients makes it perfectly possible to prepare light, delicious dishes and even create the occasional sensation, without spending hours in the kitchen.

The recipes, which use three to five ingredients, are clearly explained and extremely simple to make. You will learn to steam everything, even very rare red meat. You will make delicious, super-light, classic sauces – even mayonnaise – which will become the core of your meal when accompanied by grilled meat, vegetables or salad. You will discover that a stock based on green tea, fish cooked in paper or foil or a joint of meat cooked in water can become everyday dishes.

Have a great time in your kitchen and enjoy eating food that will keep you slim and fit.

HOW TO USE THIS BOOK

In this book I am assuming that you have at home:
- Running water
- A cooker
- A refrigerator
- A frying pan
- A cast-iron casserole
- A knife (very sharp)
- Salt and pepper
- Olive oil

(If this is not the case maybe now is the time to invest!)

The essential investment
- A steamer: ideally one with a timer, which will save you a considerable amount of time and guarantee the success of some of the recipes in this book.

What are the must-have ingredients?
- **Fresh rather than tinned:** you will find almost no tinned goods in this book, apart from indispensables like coconut milk and tomato purée.
- **Frozen:** even though you are using mainly fresh products, it is sometimes easier to buy frozen products such as peas, seafood and some fillets of fish.
- **Herbs:** there is nothing to equal fresh herbs, so choose those for preference. If you run out, you can always use the frozen or dried versions (but they are not as good).
- **Oils:** olive oil, always extra virgin (that is the best), hazelnut, sesame and walnut oils.
- **Fruit and vegetables:** be sure you use fruit and vegetables that are in season and – though this is not obligatory – preferably organic, especially lemons, because the peel is very often used.
- **Soy sauce:** preferably the Japanese Kikkoman® type, the one with the green top, which is less salty.

Which techniques should you use?
- **Cooking in a bain-marie:** this technique allows you to melt or cook a foodstuff without burning it. Place the bowl or pan containing the food inside another, larger pan of boiling water.
- **Marinating:** soaking an ingredient in an aromatic mixture to flavour or tenderize it.
- **Beating egg-whites until stiff:** add a pinch of salt to the egg-whites and use an electric mixer, gradually increasing the speed. Always beat the whites in the same direction to prevent them from going grainy.
- **Peeling an orange:** remove the peel and the white pith with a knife. Cut off both ends of the orange and gradually remove the peel by sliding the blade of the knife between the peel and the fruit, working from top to bottom.

- **Reducing:** reducing the quantity of a *jus* or stock by evaporation over heat (without the lid), while keeping it on the boil. This process concentrates the flavours and gives a smoother consistency.
- **Zesting a lemon:** There are three ways of zesting a lemon. If you are a beginner and you want a very fine zest, use a cheese grater on the peel of the lemon, going over each area just once, without touching the white pith. If you are a professional and you want zest that looks like vermicelli, use a zester. If you are resourceful and you want something like shavings, use a paring knife.

Steaming

Steaming is dull and insipid, so they say...

Dismiss this received wisdom from your mind: steaming is light, because no fat is used. It is just cooking in the oven and in water at the same time, while preserving the vitamins. This method of cooking is ideal for vegetables, fish, poultry and tender white meat. On the other hand, it is rarely recommended for red meat. However, if you follow the instructions in this book to the letter, you will be able to produce meat – even game – that is rare and juicy.

What equipment should you choose?

- **Steamer:** this is the ideal appliance for cooking without having to keep an eye on it all the time. Consisting of two or three baskets piled one on top of the other, it enables you to cook the starter and the main course at the same time.
- **Electric mixer:** its beaters are perfect for mixing sauces, beating egg-whites stiff or whipping cream. It can be replaced with a hand whisk and elbow grease!
- **Hand blender:** also known as a stick blender, this is used to mix liquids (soups, smoothies, milkshakes, etc.). It is very handy, inexpensive, space-saving, and also means less washing up, because it is used directly in whatever you are mixing with no need to transfer it to a bowl.
- **Blender:** this is more expensive than a hand blender and takes up more space but gives a smoother, creamier result – though more washing up as well, because the liquid to be mixed has to be transferred to the special bowl.
- **Multifunctional food processor:** as its name suggests, this is a multi-purpose machine. It has various tools for such functions as chopping, whisking, slicing, mincing and emulsifying.

Which gas mark?

90°C : Gas mark 3	150°C : Gas mark 5	210°C : Gas mark 7	270°C : Gas mark 9
120°C : Gas mark 4	180°C : Gas mark 6	240°C : Gas mark 8	300°C : Gas mark 10

That is everything.
All you have to do now is follow the recipe!

BREADSTICKS WITH SESAME

364 kcal/person

—

Vegetarian

—

Gluten free

Buckwheat flour
200 g

Ground almonds
80 g

Low-fat cream cheese
120 g

Sesame seeds
2 tablespoons

Preparation: 15 minutes
Cooking: 10 minutes

• Mix the **ground almonds**, **flour** and **cream cheese** to a smooth dough. Pre-heat the oven to 180°C.

• Divide the dough into small balls, shape into sticks and sprinkle with **sesame seeds**.

• Arrange the sticks in an ovenproof dish lined with baking paper and bake for 10 minutes. Serve warm, with crushed avocados.

PARSNIP HUMMUS WITH CORIANDER

68 kcal/person

—

Steam

—

Vegetarian

Parsnips
x 2

Coriander
1 bunch

Curry powder
2 tablespoons

Fromage frais
2 tablespoons

Olive oil
1 tablespoon

 Salt, pepper

Preparation: 15 minutes
Cooking: 25 minutes

• Peel the **parsnips** and steam for 25 minutes.
• Crush with a potato-masher then add the chopped **coriander**, **curry powder**, **fromage frais** and **olive oil**. Season with salt and pepper and mix. Serve cold with crudités.

PEAR SPRING ROLLS

107 kcal/person

—

Gluten free

—

Lactose free

Pears
x 2

Air-dried beef
4 slices

Rocket
100 g

Coriander
1 bunch

Rice paper wrappers
x 8 (21 cm)

Preparation: 10 minutes

• Peel the **pears** and cut into eight. Chop the **coriander** and **rocket**.

• Shortly before serving, soak the **rice paper wrappers** in a bowl of water and arrange on the worktop, smooth side down.

• Spread the other ingredients on the **rice paper wrappers**, then roll up tightly. Serve whole or cut into bite-size pieces.

PRAWN SPRING ROLLS

70 kcal/person

—

Gluten free

—

Lactose free

Cooked prawns
x 24

Kiwis
x 2

Mint
18 leaves

Coriander
1 bunch

Rice paper wrappers
x 8 (21 cm)

Preparation: 10 minutes

• Peel the **prawns**. Cut the **kiwis** into eight. Chop the **coriander** and **mint**.

• Shortly before serving, soak the **rice paper wrappers** in a bowl of water and arrange on the worktop, smooth side down.

• Spread the other ingredients on the **rice paper wrappers**, then roll up tightly. Serve whole or cut into bite-size pieces.

SALMON SPRING ROLLS

112 kcal/person

—

Gluten free

—

Lactose free

Smoked salmon
8 thin slices

Green apples
x 2

Lettuce
4 leaves

Basil
16 leaves

Rice paper wrappers
x 8 (21 cm)

Preparation: 10 minutes

• Peel the **apples** and cut into thin slices. Separate the **lettuce leaves**.

• Shortly before serving, soak the **rice paper wrappers** in a bowl of water and arrange on the worktop, smooth side down. Spread the other ingredients on the **rice paper wrappers**, then roll up tightly. Serve whole or cut into bite-size pieces.

SKATE WING RILLETTES WITH TOMATO

196 kcal/person

—

Gluten free

—

Lactose free

Skate wings
800 g

Tomatoes
x 2

Baby spinach
60 g

Wholegrain mustard
2 tablespoons

Capers in vinegar
60 g

Preparation: 25 minutes
Cooking: 20 minutes

• Remove the **spinach** stalks and roughly chop. Cut the **tomatoes** into small pieces.
• Place the **skate** in a saucepan, cover with water and cook for 20 minutes over low heat. Drain, remove the skin and cartilage, then mix the warm flesh with the remaining ingredients.
• Serve warm or cold.

16

CHICKEN AND COURGETTE SKEWERS

224 kcal/person
—
Gluten free
—
Lactose free

Chicken breasts
x 2

Courgette
x 1

Lemons
x 2

Dried thyme
1 tablespoon

Olive oil
2 tablespoons

 Salt, pepper

Preparation: 20 minutes
Marinating: 30 minutes
Cooking: 20 minutes

• Pre-heat the oven to 180°C. Cut the **chicken** in strips and slice the **courgette** in strips lengthways with a paring knife. Thread the strips onto wooden skewers and marinate for 30 minutes in the **olive oil**, grated **lemon** zest, **thyme** and **lemon** juice. Season with salt and pepper. Bake in the oven for 20 minutes. Serve hot or cold.

TAHITIAN-STYLE RAW FISH

422 kcal/person
—
Gluten free
—
Lactose free

Swordfish
600 g

Coconut milk
400 ml

Carrot
x 1 large

Limes
x 4

Coriander
1 bunch

Salt, pepper

Preparation: 15 minutes
Marinating: 5 minutes

• Cut the **fish** into cubes and squeeze the **limes**. Chop the **coriander** leaves and some of the stems, then peel the **carrot** and grate with a hand grater.
• Mix all the ingredients together in a salad bowl. Season with salt and pepper, leave to marinate for 5 minutes in the refrigerator and serve.

AUBERGINE ROULADES

129 kcal/person

—

Steam

—

Gluten free

Aubergine
x 1 large or 2 small

Fresh goats' cheese
120 g

Cooked ham
4 slices without rind

Dried thyme
3 teaspoons

 1 drizzle olive oil

🕐

Preparation: 25 minutes
Cooking: 20 minutes

- Cut the **aubergine** into 12 slices lengthways and cook for 20 minutes in a steamer.
- Mix the **goats' cheese** with the **thyme**. Cut the slices of **ham** into three.
- Place a slice of ham on each slice of **aubergine**. Spread with the cheese mixture and roll up.
- Serve with a drizzle of olive oil.

CLAMS WITH AVOCADO

187 kcal/person

—

Gluten free

—

Lactose free

Clams
x 30 (cleaned)

Avocado
x 1

Limes
x 3

Dill
1 bunch

Olive oil
1 tablespoon

Preparation: 20 minutes
Cooking: 10 minutes

• Cook the **clams** in 200 ml water over high heat until they open. Drain and strain the liquid.
• Mix the juice of the **limes** with the diced **avocado**, **olive oil**, chopped **dill** and 150 ml cooking liquid.
• Remove the upper half of the shell, arrange the **clams** on plates and garnish with the avocado mixture. Serve warm or cold.

PORK AND PRAWN NIBBLES

128 kcal/person

—

Steam

—

Gluten free

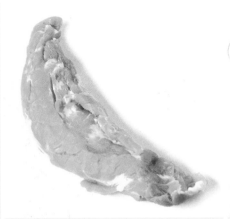

Pork fillet
300 g

Uncooked prawns
x 16 (peeled)

Egg
x 1

Sesame seeds
1 tablespoon

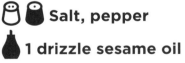 Salt, pepper

1 drizzle sesame oil

Preparation: 20 minutes
Cooking: 10 minutes

• In a blender, mix together the **pork**, half the **prawns** and the **egg**.

• Chop the remaining **prawns** and add to the mixture. Season with salt and pepper and place bite-size mounds of the mixture on squares of baking paper.

• Cook for 10 minutes in a steamer. Sprinkle with **sesame seeds** and serve warm or cold with a drizzle of sesame oil.

BASS WITH GRAPEFRUIT

194 kcal/person

—

Gluten free

—

Lactose free

Bass fillets
500 g (skinless)

Pink grapefruit
x 1

Coriander
½ bunch

Olive oil
3 tablespoons

 **Salt, pepper**

👤👤👤👤

🕑
Preparation: 15 minutes

• Squeeze the **grapefruit**, strain the juice and mix with the **olive oil**.

• Cut the **bass** into thin slices. Chop the **coriander**.

• Arrange the slices of fish on plates. Add the grapefruit juice mixture and **coriander**. Season with salt and pepper and serve.

TERRINE OF CHICKEN WITH PRESERVED LEMONS

262 kcal/person

—

Gluten free

Chicken breasts
x 2

Baby spinach
150 g

Preserved lemons
x 2

Eggs
x 2

Low-fat cream cheese
120 g

 Salt, pepper

1 drizzle olive oil for the mould

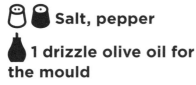

Preparation: 25 minutes
Cooking: 40 minutes

• Pre-heat the oven to 180°C. In a food processor, blend the **chicken** with the **eggs**, **cream cheese**, salt and pepper. Dice the **lemons** and add to the mixture with the **spinach**.

• Transfer to a lightly oiled non-stick mould and bake for 40 minutes.

• Turn out the hot terrine and serve cold with lettuce.

ASPARAGUS IN MOUSSELINE SAUCE

91 kcal/person

—

Vegetarian

—

Gluten free

Green asparagus
2 bunches

Egg
x 1

Mustard
1 teaspoon

Chives
1 bunch

Low-fat cream cheese
120 g

Salt, pepper

Preparation: 15 minutes
Cooking: 5 minutes

• Separate the **egg**. Mix the yolk with the **cream cheese**, **mustard** and chopped **chives** and season with salt and pepper.

• Beat the egg-white with a whisk until stiff and fold it gently into the mustard mixture. Trim the **asparagus** but do not peel, then steam for 5 minutes. Serve warm with the cold sauce.

HOT LIVER WITH CHANTERELLES

216 kcal/person

—

Gluten free

Chicken livers
250 g

Chanterelles
250 g

Eggs
x 3

Low-fat cream cheese
120 g

Thyme
4 sprigs

 **Salt, pepper**

Preparation: 20 minutes
Cooking: 25 minutes

• Pre-heat the oven to 180°C. Clean the **chanterelles** and cut into pieces.

• In a blender, mix the **chicken livers** with the **eggs**, **cream cheese**, salt and pepper. Fold in the **chanterelles** and transfer to four ramekins. Top each ramekin with a sprig of **thyme** and bake in a bain-marie for 25 minutes. Eat warm with a spoon.

WARM CARROTS WITH SAFFRON SAUCE

191 kcal/person

—

Steam

—

Vegetarian

Carrots with tops
x 16 (medium)

Eggs
x 2

Low-fat cream cheese
120 g

Powdered saffron
1 g

 Salt, pepper

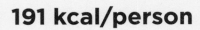

Preparation: 15 minutes
Cooking: 30 minutes

• Peel the **carrots** and cook for 30 minutes in a steamer.

• Separate the **eggs**. Mix the yolks with the **cream cheese** and the **saffron**. Season with salt and pepper.

• Before serving, beat the egg-whites until stiff, then fold into the saffron mixture. Serve the carrots warm with the cold sauce.

EGGS WITH MAYONNAISE

212 kcal/person

—

Vegetarian

—

Gluten free

Eggs
x 6 (4 whole + 2 yolks)

Strong mustard
2 tablespoons

Low-fat cream cheese
240 g

Lettuce
x 1 (small)

 **Salt, pepper**

👤👤👤👤

🕐

Preparation: 5 minutes
Cooking: 10 minutes

• Boil the **eggs** for 10 minutes, then peel.
• Beat the 2 yolks together with the **mustard** and **cream cheese**. Season with salt and pepper and serve this 'mayonnaise' with the cooled hardboiled eggs and **lettuce** leaves.

ROAST FIGS WITH AIR-DRIED BEEF

191 kcal/person

—

Gluten free

—

Lactose free

Figs
x 8

Air-dried beef
8 slices

Rosemary
4 small sprigs

 **1 drizzle olive oil**

👤👤👤👤

🕐

Preparation: 5 minutes
Cooking: 10 minutes

• Pre-heat the oven to 180°C. Make a cut in the middle of each slice of **beef** and slip the slices over the **figs**.

• Insert a sprig of **rosemary** to hold them in place and bake in the oven for 10 minutes. Serve hot with a drizzle of olive oil and a rocket salad.

STEAMED TOMATO MILLEFEUILLE

108 kcal/person

—

Steam

—

Vegetarian

Tomatoes
x 4 (medium)

Courgette
x 1

Goats' cheese
x 2 discs

Dried oregano
2 teaspoons

 Salt, pepper

1 drizzle olive oil

Preparation: 20 minutes
Cooking: 8 minutes

• Cut the **tomatoes**, cheeses and **courgette** into rounds. Season with the **oregano**, salt and pepper.
• Assemble 4 millefeuilles with layers of the various ingredients. Fix in place with a wooden cocktail stick and cook for 8 minutes in a steamer.
• Transfer the millefeuilles to plates, remove the cocktail sticks, sprinkle over some more **oregano** and serve warm with a drizzle of olive oil.

CAULIFLOWER, COCONUT AND SALMON CREAM

280 kcal/person

—

Gluten free

—

Lactose free

Cauliflower
x ½

Coconut milk
400 ml

Smoked salmon
2 slices

Grated coconut
1 tablespoon

Preparation: 15 minutes
Cooking: 35 minutes

• Cut the **cauliflower** into small pieces. Place in a saucepan with the **coconut milk** and cook for 35 minutes over low heat. Purée with a hand blender.

• Arrange the **cauliflower** cream on plates, add the **smoked salmon**, cut into pieces, sprinkle with grated **coconut** and serve.

REDUCED-FAT FOIE GRAS

339 kcal/person

—

Gluten free

—

Lactose free

Chicken livers
300 g

Fresh foie gras
150 g

Egg
x 1

Port
4 tablespoons

 Salt, pepper

👤👤👤👤

🕐

Preparation: 20 minutes
Cooking: 30 minutes
Refrigeration:
Overnight

• Pre-heat the oven to 180°C. In a food processor, blend the **chicken livers** with the **egg**, **port**, salt and pepper.

• Place the **foie gras** in the bottom of a terrine, add the blended liver, mix together, press down and bake in a bain-marie in the oven for 30 minutes.

• Leave to cool and refrigerate overnight. Eat on wholemeal toast.

CAULIFLOWER AND PRAWN CREAM

114 kcal/person

—

Gluten free

Cauliflower
x ½

Uncooked prawns
x 20 (peeled)

Paprika
1 tablespoon

Low-fat cream
400 ml

Mint
1 bunch (optional)

 1 drizzle olive oil

†††††

Preparation: 20 minutes
Cooking: 45 minutes

• Cut the **cauliflower** into pieces and cook in a saucepan with the **cream** for 40 minutes over low heat.
• Purée with a hand blender.
• Fry the **prawns** for 2 minutes in a frying pan with the olive oil and **paprika**.
• Arrange the **cauliflower** on plates. Add the **prawns** and serve with **mint** sprigs, if liked.

CHICKEN AND PRAWN TERRINE

244 kcal/person

—

Gluten free

Chicken breasts
x 2

Uncooked prawns
x 16 (peeled)

Paprika
2 tablespoons

Eggs
x 2

Low-fat cream cheese
120 g

 **Salt, pepper**

1 drizzle olive oil

Preparation: 25 minutes
Cooking: 40 minutes

• Pre-heat the oven to 180°C. In a blender, mix the **chicken** with the **eggs**, **paprika**, **cream cheese**, salt and pepper.

• Cut the **prawns** into pieces and add to the mixture. Transfer to a lightly oiled non-stick mould and bake in the oven for 40 minutes. Turn out the hot terrine and serve cold with rocket.

COCKLE AND VERBENA PARCELS

50 kcal/person

—

Gluten free

—

Lactose free

Cockles
x 60 (cleaned)

Dried verbena
2 pinches of leaves

Limes
x 2

 Salt, pepper

 **1 drizzle olive oil**

👤👤👤👤

🕐

Preparation: 10 minutes
Cooking: 10 minutes

• Pre-heat the oven to 180°C. Arrange the **cockles** and **verbena** in the centre of four pieces of baking paper. Close each parcel tightly.
• Arrange the parcels in an ovenproof dish and bake for 10 minutes. Arrange on plates and serve with **lime** wedges and a drizzle of olive oil.

SALMON, AVOCADO AND MINT TARTARE

320 kcal/person

—

Gluten free

—

Lactose free

Salmon fillets
400 g (skinless)

Avocado
x 1

Mint
20 leaves

Lemons
x 2

Olive oil
1 tablespoon

 **Salt, pepper**

⏱
Preparation: 20 minutes

• Roughly chop the **mint**.
• Dice the **salmon** and **avocado**. Add the juice of the **lemons**, **olive oil** and **mint**. Season with salt and pepper, mix and serve chilled.

STUFFED MUSHROOMS WITH FROMAGE FRAIS

165 kcal/person

Closed-cup mushrooms
x 8 (large)

Smoked duck breast
8 slices

Fromage frais
100 g

Soy sauce
2 tablespoons

Dried thyme
1 teaspoon

 Salt, pepper

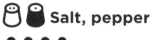

Preparation: 20 minutes
Cooking: 25 minutes

• Pre-heat the oven to 180°C. Remove the **mushroom** stalks and chop finely. Remove the fat from the **duck breast** and dice the meat.

• Mix the **duck** with the **cheese**, **thyme** and the chopped **mushroom** stalks. Season with salt and pepper and fill the **mushroom** cups with the mixture.

• Drizzle with **soy sauce** and bake in the oven for 25 minutes.

TROUT TARTARE

197 kcal/person

—

Gluten free

Smoked trout
4 slices

Trout roe
100 g

Lime
x 1

Salmon trout fillets
400 g (skinless)

Fromage frais
1 tablespoon

Preparation: 10 minutes

• Cut the **smoked trout** and **salmon trout** into small, even-sized pieces. Mix with the **roe**, **fromage frais** and **lime** juice. Serve chilled on Swedish crispbread.

PASSION FRUIT AND PRAWN CEVICHE

30 kcal/person

—

Lactose free

Passion fruit
x 4 (large)

Cooked prawns
x 8

Coriander
½ bunch

Soy sauce
4 tablespoons

Olive oil
1 tablespoon

 Salt, pepper

🕐

Preparation: 15 minutes

• Peel and cut the **prawns** into small pieces. Chop the **coriander**.

• Cut the **passion fruit** in half, scoop out the pulp and mix it with the remaining ingredients. Serve in the fruit skins or in bowls, season with salt and pepper and enjoy.

LEEKS VINAIGRETTE

78 kcal/person

—

Vegetarian

—

Gluten free

Leeks
x 2

Wholegrain mustard
2 tablespoons

Balsamic vinegar
2 tablespoons

Greek-style yoghurt
300 g

Chives
1 bunch

Salt, pepper

Preparation: 15 minutes
Cooking: 40 minutes

• Cut the **leeks** in three lengthways, then in half crossways. Wash under cold running water and cook in a steamer for 40 minutes.
• Mix the **yoghurt** with the **mustard**, chopped **chives** and **vinegar**. Season with salt and pepper and serve the **leeks** warm with the sauce.

SALMON IN A LEMON AND MINT MARINADE

223 kcal/person

—

Gluten free

—

Lactose free

Salmon fillets
400 g (skinless)

Lemons
x 2

Mint
10 leaves

Olive oil
2 tablespoons

Salt, pepper

Preparation: 10 minutes
Marinating: 5 minutes

• Cut the **salmon** into very thin slices and arrange on small individual plates.
• Add the juice of the **lemons**, **olive oil** and **mint**. Season with salt and pepper, leave to marinate for 5 minutes and serve.

ASPARAGUS MIMOSA

272 kcal/person

—

Vegetarian

—

Gluten free

Green asparagus
x 20

Eggs
x 2

Cornichons
x 16

Chervil
1 bunch

Capers
80 g

 **Salt, pepper**

Preparation: 10 minutes
Cooking: 20 minutes

• Chop the **chervil** and **cornichons**. Boil the **eggs** for 10 minutes and peel.

• 15 minutes before serving, trim the **asparagus** and steam for 10 minutes. Place in a serving dish, add the **capers**, **chervil** and **cornichons**. Grate over the **eggs**. Season with salt and pepper and serve warm.

STEAMED TOMATOES FILLED WITH TUNA

73 kcal/person

—

Steam

—

Gluten free

Tomatoes
x 4

Black olives
x 16 (stoned)

Dried thyme
2 teaspoons

Fromage frais
150 g

Tuna in its own juice
1 x 160 g tin

 Salt, pepper

1 drizzle olive oil

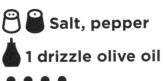

Preparation: 20 minutes
Cooking: 5 minutes

• Cut the **tomatoes** in half and scoop out the insides. Mix the fromage frais with the flaked **tuna**, chopped **olives** and **thyme**. Season with salt and pepper.

• Fill the **tomatoes** with the mixture and cook for 5 minutes in a steamer. Serve hot or cold with a drizzle of olive oil.

MACKEREL AND TOMATOES IN WHITE WINE

90 kcal/person

—

Gluten free

—

Lactose free

Mackerel
4 fillets

White wine
400 ml

Cherry tomatoes
200 g

Bouquet garni
x 1

Star anise
x 3

Preparation: 10 minutes
Cooking: 25 minutes
Refrigeration:
Overnight

• Pre-heat the oven to 180°C. Place the **mackerel** in a large gratin dish. Add the halved **tomatoes**.
• Heat the **white wine** with the **star anise**, **bouquet garni** and 100 ml water for 10 minutes over medium heat. Pour the boiling liquid over the mackerel. Bake in the oven for 15 minutes. Leave to cool and refrigerate overnight. Serve cold.

SEA BREAM AND PINEAPPLE TARTARE

252 kcal/person

—

Gluten free

—

Lactose free

Mini pineapples
x 2

Sea bream
4 fillets (skinless)

Limes
x 2

Coriander
1 bunch

Olive oil
2 tablespoons

 **Salt, pepper**

Preparation: 20 minutes

• Cut the **pineapples** in half. Scoop out the flesh and cut into small pieces. Cut the **sea bream** into cubes. Squeeze the **limes**. Roughly chop the **coriander**. Mix all the ingredients together, season with salt and pepper, arrange in the **pineapple** halves and serve.

MELON AND SALMON SASHIMI

330 kcal/person

—

Lactose free

Cantaloupe melon
x 1 (small)

Salmon steaks
x 3 (150 g each, skinless)

Soy sauce
4 tablespoons

Wasabi
1 teaspoon

 Grey sea salt

Preparation: 10 minutes
Refrigeration:
20 minutes

• Cover the **salmon** with grey sea salt and refrigerate for 20 minutes. Rinse the **salmon steaks** in cold water and cut into pieces.
• Peel the **melon** and cut into pieces the same size as the pieces of **salmon**. Arrange together in a serving dish.
• Mix the **wasabi** with the **soy sauce**, pour over and serve.

SCALLOP CARPACCIO

158 kcal/person

—

Gluten free

—

Lactose free

Scallops
x 12 (without coral)

Cucumber
x 1 (about 200 g)

Raspberries
x 16

Limes
x 2

Olive oil
2 tablespoons

 Salt, pepper

Preparation: 15 minutes
Marinating: 5 minutes

• Cut the **cucumber** into thin slices.
• Slice the **scallops** and mix with the zest and juice of the **limes**, the **olive oil** and the crushed **raspberries**. Season with salt and pepper.
• Leave to marinate for 5 minutes. Arrange the scallop mixture and **cucumber** on a plate and serve.

OYSTERS WITH MANDARIN JUICE AND BASIL

137 kcal/person

—

Lactose free

Oysters
x 24 (small)

Mandarins
x 6

Basil
24 leaves

Soy sauce
24 drops

Olive oil
24 drops

 **24 pinches pepper**

Grey sea salt

♟♟♟♟

🕐

Preparation: 10 minutes
Cooking: 5 minutes

• Pre-heat the oven to 180°C. Squeeze the **mandarins** and reserve the juice.
• Bake the **oysters** in the oven for 5 minutes. Allow to cool before opening. Pour off the oyster liquor and arrange the **oysters** on a bed of salt. Refrigerate.
• 2 minutes before serving, put a **basil** leaf on each **oyster**. Add the mandarin juice, **olive oil**, **soy sauce** and pepper to each oyster.

OYSTERS WITH MANGO AND CORIANDER

108 kcal/person
—
Lactose free

Oysters
x 24 (small)

Mango
x ½ (not too ripe)

Shallot
x 1 (or 2 small)

Coriander
6 sprigs

Vinegar
24 drops

Grey sea salt

24 drops of olive oil

Preparation: 10 minutes
Cooking: 5 minutes

• Pre-heat the oven to 180°C. Dice the **shallot** and the **mango**. Chop the **coriander**. Bake the **oysters** in the oven for 5 minutes. Allow to cool before opening. Pour off the oyster liquor and arrange the **oysters** on a bed of salt. Refrigerate.
• Mix together the **mango**, **shallot**, olive oil, **vinegar** and **coriander** and top the **oysters** with it

CAESAR SALAD

351 kcal/person

—

Steam

Little Gem lettuces
x 4

Chicken breasts
600 g

Grated Parmesan
4 tablespoons

Fromage frais
4 tablespoons

Swedish crispbread
2 slices

 **Salt, pepper**

👫👫

🕐
Preparation: 10 minutes
Cooking: 20 minutes

• Cook the **chicken breasts** for 20 minutes in a steamer or in boiling water and cut into pieces. Separate the **lettuce** leaves.
• Break the **crispbread** into pieces.
• Mix all the ingredients in a salad bowl. Season with salt and pepper and serve.

AUBERGINE SALAD

79 kcal/person

—

Vegetarian

—

Gluten free

Aubergines
x 2 (medium)

Tomatoes
x 3

Black olives
x 20 (stoned)

Basil
1 bunch (50 g)

Olive oil
2 tablespoons

 **Salt, pepper**

🏃🏃🏃🏃

🕐

Preparation: 10 minutes
Cooking: 40 minutes

• Cook the **aubergines** whole for 40 minutes in a steamer and allow to cool.
• Cut the **tomatoes** and **olives** into pieces and chop the **basil**. Cut open the **aubergines**, scoop out the flesh with a spoon and mix with the other ingredients. Season with salt and pepper and serve.

BEEF, LAMB'S LETTUCE AND TURMERIC SALAD

192 kcal/person

—

Steam

Fillet of beef
400 g

Lamb's lettuce
150 g

Turmeric
1 tablespoon

Greek-style yoghurt
150 g

 **Salt, pepper**

☖☖☖☖

⏱

Preparation: 15 minutes
Cooking: 8 minutes

• Cook the **fillet of beef** for 8 minutes in a steamer. Allow to cool, then cut the meat into thin slices and mix with the **lamb's lettuce**, **yoghurt** and **turmeric**. Season with salt and pepper and serve.

86

BROCCOLI AND DRIED FRUIT SALAD

60 kcal/person

—

Steam

—

Vegetarian

Broccoli
500 g

Dried apricots
x 8

Walnut halves
x 8

Flaked almonds
2 tablespoons

Hazelnuts
x 16

Salt, pepper

1 drizzle hazelnut oil

Preparation: 15 minutes
Cooking: 10 minutes

• Cut the **broccoli** into pieces and cook for 10 minutes in a steamer.
• In a salad bowl, mix the **broccoli** with the **almonds**, the **apricots**, cut into pieces, and the chopped **walnuts** and **hazelnuts**. Season with salt and pepper and serve with a drizzle of hazelnut oil.

LENTIL AND PRAWN SALAD

230 kcal/person

—

Gluten free

—

Lactose free

Green lentils
250 g

Cooked prawns
x 16 (peeled)

Tarragon
1 bunch

Clementines
x 4

Olive oil
2 tablespoons

 Salt, pepper

Preparation: 15 minutes
Cooking: 25 minutes

• Cook the **lentils** for 25 minutes in a large quantity of water. Drain, tip into a salad bowl and leave to cool.

• Add the **prawns**, cut into pieces, the juice of the **clementines**, the chopped **tarragon** and the **olive oil**. Season with salt and pepper, mix and serve.

PINEAPPLE AND CHICKEN SALAD

334 kcal/person

—

Steam

—

Gluten free

Chicken breasts
x 3

Mini pineapple
x 1

Rocket
150 g

Greek-style yoghurt
150 g

Cider vinegar
1 tablespoon

 **Salt, pepper**

Preparation: 15 minutes
Cooking: 20 minutes

• Cook the **chicken breasts** for 20 minutes in a steamer or in boiling water. Leave to cool and cut into pieces.

• Skin the **pineapple** and cut into cubes. Mix all the ingredients together in a salad bowl. Season with salt and pepper and serve immediately.

BEEF SALAD WITH RASPBERRIES

191 kcal/person

—

Gluten free

Fillet or rib steak
400 g

Rocket
120 g

Raspberries
125 g

Balsamic vinegar
2 tablespoons

Greek-style yoghurt
150 g

 Salt, pepper

Preparation: 20 minutes
Cooking: 30 seconds

• Halve the **raspberries**.
• Cut the **steak** into cubes and seal for 30 seconds in a very hot dry pan, stirring continuously.
• Put the meat in a salad bowl with the other ingredients. Season with salt and pepper, mix and serve immediately.

VEAL SALAD WITH BLUEBERRIES

160 kcal/person

—

Gluten free

Veal escalopes
x 2

Blueberries
125 g

Greek-style yoghurt
150 g

Rocket
120 g

Mustard
1 tablespoon

 **Salt, pepper**

Preparation: 15 minutes
Cooking: 1 minute

- Cut the **veal** into small pieces and seal for 1 minute in a very hot dry pan, stirring continuously.
- Put the meat in a salad bowl with the other ingredients. Season with salt and pepper, mix and serve immediately.

APPLES WITH HOT GOATS' CHEESE

325 kcal/person

—

Vegetarian

—

Gluten free

Goats' cheese
x 2 discs

Apples
x 2

Walnut halves
x 12

Rocket
100 g

Liquid honey
2 tablespoons

 1 drizzle walnut oil

👤👤👤👤

🕐

Preparation: 10 minutes
Cooking: 15 minutes

• Pre-heat the oven to 180°C. Peel the **apples**, cut in half and remove the cores. Put half a **cheese** on each **apple** half, cover with **honey** and bake in the oven for 15 minutes.

• Chop the **walnuts**. Arrange the hot **cheese** and **apple** on a bed of **rocket** leaves, add the **walnuts** and serve with a drizzle of walnut oil.

OCTOPUS SALAD

213 kcal/person

—

Gluten free

—

Lactose free

Octopus
x 1 (1 kg)

Coriander
2 bunches

Limes
x 2

Paprika
1 tablespoon

Olive oil
2 tablespoons

Preparation: 15 minutes
Cooking: 20 minutes

• Squeeze the **limes** and chop the **coriander**.
• Place the **octopus** in a casserole, cover with water and bring to the boil. Cook for 20 minutes, then take off the heat. Leave to cool in the casserole.
• Cut the **octopus** into pieces and mix with the remaining ingredients. Serve immediately.

GREEN TOMATOES WITH MOZZARELLA

175 kcal/person

—

Vegetarian

—

Gluten free

Green tomatoes
x 4

Mozzarella
150 g

Pine nuts
2 tablespoons

Basil
2 bunches

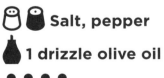 **Salt, pepper**

1 drizzle olive oil

Preparation: 10 minutes
Cooking: 10 minutes

• Pre-heat the oven to 180°C. Chop the **basil**.
• Cut the **tomatoes** in half and place a piece of **mozzarella** on each half. Bake in the oven for 10 minutes.
• Arrange the **tomatoes** in a serving dish. Add the **basil** and the **pine nuts**, season with salt and pepper and serve warm with a drizzle of olive oil.

GRATED CARROTS WITH CORIANDER

47 kcal/person

—

Vegetarian

—

Lactose free

Carrots
3 (large, about 450 g)

Clementines
x 2

Soy sauce
3 tablespoons

Coriander
1 bunch

 Salt, pepper

Preparation: 15 minutes

• Chop the **coriander**. Squeeze the **clementines**.
• Grate the **carrots** and mix with the remaining ingredients. Season with salt and pepper and serve.

TOMATO SALAD WITH HERBS

94 kcal/person

—

Vegetarian

—

Gluten free

Tomatoes
x 9 (medium)

Basil
1 bunch

Tarragon
1 bunch

Low-fat cream cheese
120 g

 Salt, pepper

Preparation: 15 minutes

• Pick off the leaves of the **basil** and **tarragon**. In a blender, mix three-quarters of the herbs with the **cream cheese** and 20 ml water.

• Mix this sauce with the **tomatoes**, cut into pieces. Add the remaining herbs. Season with salt and pepper and serve.

BRUSSELS SPROUT SALAD

145 kcal/person

—

Steam

—

Gluten free

Brussels sprouts
x 24

Hazelnut oil
1 tablespoon

Hazelnuts
x 12

Air-dried beef
4 thin slices

 Salt, pepper

Preparation: 15 minutes
Cooking: 15 minutes

• Cut the **air-dried beef** into small strips. Roughly chop the **hazelnuts**.

• Steam the **Brussels sprouts** for 15 minutes. Mix with the beef strips and **hazelnuts**, drizzle with hazelnut oil, season with salt and pepper and serve hot or cold.

MUSSEL SALAD

360 kcal/person

—

Gluten free

—

Lactose free

Mussels
3 litres (cleaned)

Cucumber
x ½ (250 g)

Peas
300 g

Lamb's lettuce
150 g

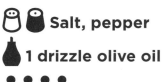 **Salt, pepper**

 1 drizzle olive oil

Preparation: 20 minutes
Cooking: 15 minutes

• Place the **mussels** in a saucepan over high heat and stir continuously until they are open. Strain any cooking juices and set aside. Remove the mussels from the shells.

• In a blender, mix three-quarters of the **peas**, the olive oil, half the **cucumber** and the cooking juices.

• Mix everything together with the remainder of the **cucumber**, peeled and sliced, the **peas** and the **lamb's lettuce**. Season with salt and pepper.

CAULIFLOWER TABBOULEH

43 kcal/person

—

Steam

—

Vegetarian

Cauliflower
x 1

Tomatoes
x 2

Mint
1 bunch

Cucumber
x ½ (250 g)

Salt, pepper

Preparation: 15 minutes
Cooking: 10 minutes

• Chop the **mint**.
• Remove the stalk and leaves of the **cauliflower** and grate the **cauliflower** by hand. Place the grated **cauliflower** on a sheet of moistened baking paper and cook for 10 minutes in a steamer.
• Mix the **cauliflower** 'couscous' with the diced **cucumber** and **tomatoes** and the **mint**. Season with salt and pepper and serve.

PEA GAZPACHO

92 kcal/person

—

Vegetarian

—

Lactose free

Peas
500 g (frozen or fresh)

Cucumber
400 g

Mint
1 bunch

Olive oil
12 drops

 Salt, pepper

Preparation: 20 minutes
Cooking: 5 minutes

• Chop the **mint**.
• Cook the **peas** for 5 minutes in boiling water, then drain.
• In a blender, mix the **peas** with the diced **cucumber**, 100 ml water and the **olive oil**. Season, add the mint and serve chilled.

ARTICHOKE AND CUCUMBER GAZPACHO

130 kcal/person

—

Vegetarian

—

Lactose free

Artichoke bottoms
x 8

Cucumber
400 g

Olive oil
2 tablespoons

  Salt, pepper

Preparation: 10 minutes
Cooking: 30 minutes

• Dice the **cucumber**. Cook the **artichoke bottoms** for 30 minutes in boiling salted water. Drain and leave to cool.

• Blend the **artichoke bottoms** with half the **cucumber**, 50 ml water and the **olive oil**.

• Season with salt and pepper and pour into bowls. Add the remaining diced cucumber and serve chilled.

MELON, TOMATO AND MINT GAZPACHO

110 kcal/person

—

Gluten free

—

Lactose free

Cantaloupe melon
x 1

Tomatoes
x 4 (medium)

Mint
1 bunch

Olive oil
2 tablespoons

 **Salt, pepper**

Preparation: 10 minutes

• Chop the **mint** (reserve a few small leaves). Halve the **tomatoes**, scoop out the insides and chop. Peel and de-seed the **melon**.
• In a blender, mix the **melon**, **tomatoes**, **mint**, 20 ml water and the **olive oil**. Season with salt and pepper and refrigerate.
• Transfer to bowls, add the **mint** leaves and serve.

WATERMELON AND TOMATO GAZPACHO

98 kcal/person

—

Vegetarian

—

Gluten free

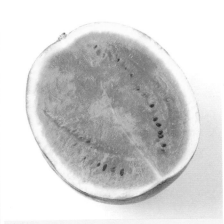
Watermelon
850 g

Cherry tomatoes
250 g

Mint
1 bunch

   Salt, pepper

 1 drizzle olive oil

🕐
Preparation: 10 minutes

• Chop the **mint** (reserve a few small leaves). Cut the **tomatoes** in half. De-seed and chop the watermelon.

• In a blender, mix the **watermelon** with three-quarters of the **tomatoes**, 20 ml water and the mint. Season with salt and pepper and refrigerate.

• Transfer the gazpacho to bowls. Add the remaining tomatoes, the **mint** leaves and a drizzle of olive oil.

MELON, FETA AND OREGANO GAZPACHO

175 kcal/person

—

Vegetarian

—

Gluten free

Cantaloupe melons
x 2

Dried oregano
4 teaspoons

Feta
100 g

 **Salt, pepper**

1 drizzle olive oil

Preparation: 10 minutes

• Peel and de-seed the **melons**. Cut about 4 tablespoons of flesh into small cubes. Crush the **feta** with a fork.

• In a blender, mix the remaining **melon** flesh with 50 ml water and the **oregano**. Season with salt and pepper and refrigerate.

• Transfer the gazpacho to bowls. Add the feta, the melon cubes and a drizzle of olive oil. Serve chilled.

VEGETABLE BOUILLON WITH SALMON

167 kcal/person

—

Gluten free

—

Lactose free

Salmon steaks
x 2 (skinless)

Peas
150 g

Celeriac
300 g

Carrots
300 g

Closed-cup mushrooms
100 g

Preparation: 15 minutes
Cooking: 45 minutes

• Peel and dice the **carrots** and **celeriac**. Cook for 45 minutes over low heat in 1.5 litres of water. Add the **peas** half-way through cooking.

• Cut the **mushrooms** and **salmon** into small pieces and arrange together in bowls. Pour over the piping hot bouillon and leave to stand for 1 minute before serving.

GREEN TEA, SALMON AND GRAPEFRUIT

180 kcal/person

—

Gluten free

—

Lactose free

Salmon fillets
250 g (skinless)

Pink grapefruit
x 2

Jasmine green tea
400 ml (cold)

Kiwis
x 2

Coriander
12 sprigs

 Grey sea salt

👤👤👤👤

🕐

Preparation: 20 minutes
Refrigeration:
40 minutes

• Cover the **salmon** with coarse grey salt. Refrigerate for 40 minutes.
• Squeeze the **grapefruit** to give 200 ml juice. Mix with the tea.
• Rinse the **salmon** in cold water and cut into cubes. Divide into bowls and top with the chopped **kiwis** and the **coriander**. Pour over the tea and juice mixture and serve.

BEEF BOUILLON WITH LEMON GRASS

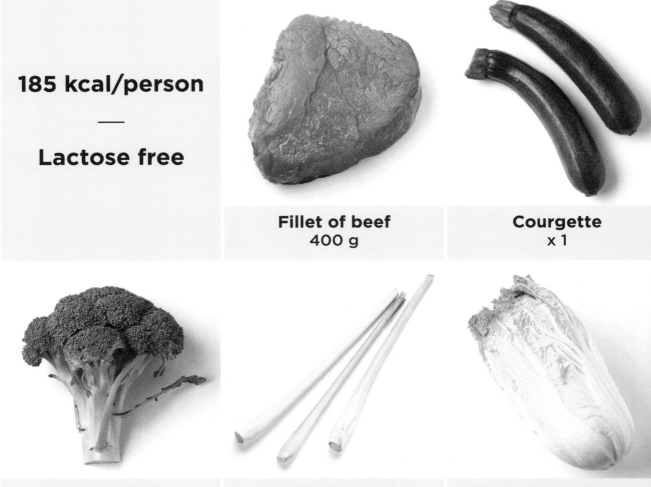

185 kcal/person
—
Lactose free

Fillet of beef
400 g

Courgette
x 1

Broccoli
100 g

Lemon grass
2 stems

Chinese cabbage
400 g

 1 drizzle soy sauce

👤👤👤👤

🕐

Preparation: 15 minutes
Cooking: 40 minutes

• Cook the thinly sliced **Chinese cabbage**, sliced **lemon grass**, chopped **broccoli** and the **courgette**, cut into rounds, in a saucepan with 1.5 litres of water for 40 minutes over low heat.
• Cut the meat into small cubes and divide into bowls. Pour over the piping hot bouillon and stand for 1 minute. Serve with a drizzle of soy sauce.

BUTTERNUT SQUASH SOUP WITH WALNUTS

80 kcal/person

—

Vegetarian

—

Lactose free

Butternut squash
x 1 (about 600 g)

Carrots
x 2

Walnut halves
x 8

Sweet onion
x 1

Walnut oil
1 tablespoon

 Salt, pepper

Preparation: 20 minutes
Cooking: 45 minutes

• Peel the **squash**, **carrots** and **onion** into big chunks. Place in a casserole, add water to 1 cm above the vegetables and cook for 45 minutes over low heat. Purée with a hand blender.

• Season with salt and pepper and transfer to bowls. Add the chopped **walnuts** and a few drops of the **walnut oil** to each bowl and serve.

BEEF BOUILLON WITH TEA

138 kcal/person

—

Lactose free

Fillet of beef
200 g

Basil
20 leaves

Earl Grey tea
400 ml (hot)

Cucumber
100 g

Green asparagus
x 8

🧂 **Grey sea salt**

🚶🚶🚶🚶

🕐

Preparation: 10 minutes
Refrigeration:
40 minutes

• Cover the **beef** with coarse grey sea salt. Refrigerate for 40 minutes.

• Trim the **asparagus** and cut into small cubes. Dice the **cucumber**.

• Rinse the **beef** in cold water. Cut into cubes and divide into bowls with the **asparagus**, **cucumber** and chopped **basil**. Pour over the boiling hot **tea**, stand for 1 minute and serve.

BEEF AND CARROT BOUILLON

130 kcal/person

—

Gluten free

—

Lactose free

Carrots
500 g

Fillet of beef
250 g

Tarragon
1 bunch

Turnips
250 g

 Salt, pepper

Preparation: **10 minutes**
Cooking: **45 minutes**

• Cut the **carrots** and **turnips** into small even-sized cubes and cook for 45 minutes over low heat in 1 litre of water. Take off the heat and add the **beef**, cut into small pieces.

• Leave to stand for 5 minutes in the hot bouillon. Season with salt and pepper, add the chopped **tarragon** and serve.

RATATOUILLE AND CHORIZO BOUILLON

53 kcal/person

—

Gluten free

—

Lactose free

Red pepper
x 1

Courgettes
x 2

Chorizo
4 thin slices

Tomatoes
x 2

Basil
1 bunch

 Salt, pepper

Preparation: 25 minutes
Cooking: 45 minutes

• De-seed and dice the **pepper** and **tomatoes**. Cook for 45 minutes over low heat in a casserole with 1.5 litres of water.

• Chop the **basil**, cut the **chorizo** into strips. Mix the **basil** and **chorizo** into the bouillon. Season with salt and pepper and serve.

TURKEY BOUILLON WITH FENNEL

138 kcal/person

—

Gluten free

—

Lactose free

Turkey escalopes
x 3 (150 g each)

Cherry tomatoes
x 20

Dill
1 bunch

Fennel seeds
1 tablespoon

Fennel
2 bulbs

 **Salt, pepper**

👤👤👤👤

🕐
Preparation: 20 minutes
Cooking: 1 hour

• Cut the **turkey escalopes** into small pieces. Cut the **fennel** into pieces and cook with the **turkey** pieces in a casserole with 1.5 litres of water for 1 hour over low heat.

• Add the **cherry tomatoes** and **fennel seeds** 10 minutes before the end of cooking time. Season with salt and pepper and transfer to bowls. Add the chopped **dill**, leave to stand for 1 minute and serve.

SCALLOP BOUILLON WITH CELERY

44 kcal/person

—

Gluten free

—

Lactose free

Scallops
x 12

Celery
1 stick

Pink grapefruit
x 2

Baby spinach
100 g

Lemon grass
2 stems

 Salt, pepper

Preparation: 20 minutes
Cooking: 25 minutes

• Trim and slice the **celery** and slice the **lemon grass**. Cook for 25 minutes in 1.5 litres of water over low heat. Squeeze the **grapefruit** and strain the juice.

• Remove the stalks from the **spinach**. Add to the bouillon with the **scallops**. Take off the heat and leave to cool. Add the **grapefruit** juice, season with salt and pepper and serve.

THAI SOUP WITH CHICKEN AND PRAWNS

600 kcal/person

—

Gluten free

—

Lactose free

Chicken breasts
x 2

Closed-cup mushrooms
500 g

Uncooked prawns
x 12 (peeled)

Lemon grass
2 stems

Coconut milk
800 ml

Salt, pepper

Preparation: 25 minutes
Cooking: 46 minutes

• Cut the **chicken** and **mushrooms** into pieces and slice the **lemon grass**. Cook in a casserole with the **coconut milk** for 45 minutes over low heat.
• Add the **prawns** and cook for a further 1 minute. Season with salt and pepper. Serve with fresh coriander, if liked.

FISH CONSOMMÉ WITH GREEN TEA

140 kcal/person

—

Gluten free

—

Lactose free

Cod
350 g

Black olives
x 12 (stoned)

Tarragon
1 bunch

Clementines
x 4

Jasmine green tea
500 ml (cold)

Preparation: 10 minutes
Cooking: 5 minutes

• Steam or boil the **cod** for 5 minutes. Divide into bowls, add the **olives**, cut into pieces, and the chopped **tarragon**.
• Mix the strained juice of the **clementines** with the cold **tea**. Pour into the bowls and serve.

PRAWN BOUILLON WITH GINGER

64 kcal/person

—

Lactose free

Chinese cabbage
400 g

Uncooked prawns
x 24 (peeled)

Fresh ginger
50 g

Anise seeds
2 tablespoons

Soy sauce
4 tablespoons

Preparation: 20 minutes
Cooking: 46 minutes

• In a casserole, cook the thinly sliced **Chinese cabbage**, the **ginger**, peeled and cut into thin rounds, and the **anise seeds** in 1.5 litres of water for 45 minutes over low heat.

• Add the **prawns** and the **soy sauce**. Cook for a further 1 minute and serve.

CREAMY SALMON AND SPINACH SOUP

435 kcal/person

—

Gluten free

—

Lactose free

Baby spinach
300 g

Coconut milk
800 ml

Celeriac
150 g

Smoked salmon
4 slices

 **Salt, pepper**

👤👤👤👤

🕐

Preparation: 20 minutes
Cooking: 20 minutes

• Trim the **spinach** and reserve about 20 small leaves. Cook for 20 minutes over low heat in a casserole with the **coconut milk**, the **celeriac** cut into pieces and 500 ml water.

• Purée with a hand blender. Season with salt and pepper and arrange in bowls. Add the **spinach** and the **salmon**, cut into small pieces. Serve.

VEGETABLE MINESTRONE

64 kcal/person

—

Vegetarian

—

Gluten free

Peas
150 g

Cherry tomatoes
x 8

Celeriac
300 g

Carrots
300 g

Green beans
100 g

 **Salt, pepper**

 1 drizzle olive oil

Preparation: 20 minutes
Cooking: 50 minutes

• Peel and dice the **celeriac** and **carrots** and cut the **beans** into small pieces. Cook for 45 minutes over low heat in 1.5 litres of water.

• Add the **peas** and the halved **tomatoes** and cook for a further 5 minutes. Season with salt and pepper and serve with a few drops of olive oil.

CHICKEN BOUILLON WITH GINGER

282 kcal/person

—

Lactose free

Chicken breasts
x 3

Cherry tomatoes
250 g

Fresh ginger
80 g

Basil
1 bunch

Soy sauce
4 tablespoons

Preparation: 20 minutes
Cooking: 45 minutes

• In a casserole, cook the **chicken**, cut into pieces, the peeled and grated **ginger** and the halved **tomatoes** in 1.5 litres of water for 45 minutes over low heat.

• Pick and chop the **basil** leaves. Add to the bouillon with the **soy sauce**. Mix and serve.

CABBAGE SOUP WITH HADDOCK

175 kcal/person

—

Gluten free

—

Lactose free

Haddock
1 fillet (350 g)

Savoy cabbage
500 g

Sweet onion
x 1

Bouquet garni
x 1

Carrots
x 2

 Salt, pepper

Preparation: 15 minutes
Cooking: 1 hour

• In a casserole, cook the thinly sliced **onion**, the **cabbage**, cut into pieces, the **carrots**, cut into rounds, and the **bouquet garni** in 1.5 litres of water for 55 minutes over low heat.

• Add the **haddock**, cut into pieces, and cook for a further 5 minutes. Season with salt and pepper and serve.

SCALLOPS IN VANILLA BOUILLON

Scallops
x 12 (with or without coral)

Vanilla
3 pods

Leeks
x 2 (small)

Pink grapefruit
x 1

Preparation: 15 minutes
Cooking: 23 minutes

• Split open the **vanilla** pods, scrape out and reserve the seeds. Squeeze the **grapefruit** and strain the juice to give 100 ml.

• Wash the **leeks**, slice thinly and cook with the **vanilla** pods in 1.5 litres of water for 15 minutes over low heat. Add the **scallops**, cut into pieces, and cook for a further 8 minutes. Serve in bowls, topped with the **grapefruit** juice and **vanilla** seeds.

AVOCADO AND PEAR BOUILLON

162 kcal/person

—

Vegetarian

—

Gluten free

Pears
x 2

Avocado
x 1

Green tea with lemon
500 ml (cold)

Basil
16 leaves

Pink grapefruit
x 2

 Pepper

Preparation: 20 minutes

• Squeeze the **grapefruit** and strain the juice to give 200 ml and mix this with the cold **tea**.
• Just before serving, cut the **pears** and **avocado** into pieces, chop the **basil** and arrange in bowls. Add the tea and grapefruit juice mixture, season lightly with pepper and serve.

CREAM OF ARTICHOKE WITH SOFT-BOILED EGGS

217 kcal/person

—

Gluten free

Artichoke bottoms
x 8

Eggs
x 4

Air-dried beef
4 slices

Low-fat cream cheese
120 g

 Salt, pepper

Preparation: 15 minutes
Cooking: 35 minutes

• Cook the **artichoke bottoms** for 30 minutes in boiling salted water. In a blender, mix with the **cream cheese** and 50 ml water. Season with salt and pepper.

• Cut the **air-dried beef** into thin strips. Boil the **eggs** for exactly 5 minutes then peel in cold water.

• Transfer the artichoke cream to plates, add the **beef** strips and the halved **eggs**.

BEEF BOUILLON WITH MUSHROOMS

117 kcal/person

—

Gluten free

—

Lactose free

Fillet or rib steak
200 g

Closed-cup mushrooms
150 g

Turnips
200 g

Carrots
250 g

Thyme
1 tablespoon

Preparation: 15 minutes
Cooking: 45 minutes

• In a casserole, cook the diced **turnips**, diced **carrots** and **thyme** in 1.5 litres of water for 45 minutes over low heat.
• Cut the **mushrooms** and **steak** into small pieces and divide into bowls. Pour over the piping hot bouillon, leave to stand for 1 minute and serve.

CREAM OF SPINACH, CELERY AND PRAWNS

217 kcal/person

—

Gluten free

—

Lactose free

Celery
2 sticks

Coconut milk
400 ml

Coriander
12 sprigs

Uncooked prawns
x 16 (peeled)

Fresh spinach
100 g

 **Salt, pepper**

Preparation: 10 minutes
Cooking: 47 minutes

• In a casserole, cook the **spinach** and the chopped **celery** for 45 minutes over low heat with the **coconut milk** and 100 ml water. Purée with a hand blender and season with salt and pepper.
• Add the **prawns** and cook for a further 2 minutes. Transfer to bowls, add the **coriander** and serve.

SEAFOOD WITH GREEN TEA

131 kcal/person

—

Gluten free

—

Lactose free

Cooked prawns
x 12

Oysters
x 12 (medium)

Cherry tomatoes
x 8

Lemon thyme
4 sprigs

Jasmine green tea
500 ml

Preparation: 15 minutes
Cooking: 5 minutes

• Bake the **oysters** in the oven for 5 minutes at 180°C, open them up and divide into bowls. Mix the liquor from the **oysters** with the **tea** and **thyme**. Heat and allow to stand for 5 minutes, strain and leave to cool.

• Peel the **prawns** and add to the bowls along with the chopped **tomatoes**. Pour over the **tea** and serve.

DUCK BOUILLON WITH SAGE

66 kcal/person

—

Lactose free

Duck fillets
x 4

Closed-cup mushrooms
600 g

Sage
18 leaves

Soy sauce
4 tablespoons

Preparation: 15 minutes
Cooking: 30 minutes

• Thinly slice the **mushrooms** and **sage**. Place in a saucepan, add 1.5 litres of water and cook for 30 minutes over low heat.

• Slice the **duck** into thin strips and divide into bowls with the **soy sauce**. Pour over the piping hot bouillon, leave to stand for 1 minute and serve.

TARTARE SAUCE

44 kcal/person

To serve with:
Poached or steamed fish
Grilled meat or fish
Grated red or white cabbage
Steamed vegetables
Poached or steamed poultry
Raw minced beef
Raw vegetable sticks
Omelettes
Salads

Tarragon
1 bunch

Mustard
1 tablespoon

Chives
1 bunch

Low-fat cream cheese
120 g

Capers
60 g

 **Salt, pepper**

 Preparation: 15 minutes

• Mix together the **cream cheese**, **mustard** and roughly chopped **capers**.

• Add the chopped **tarragon** and **chives**. Season with salt and pepper and serve.

SAUCE VIERGE

94 kcal/person

To serve with:
Meat
Fish
Grilled poultry
Steamed vegetables
Salads
Raw vegetables
Steamed fish, shellfish or poultry
White beans
Lentils

Tomatoes
x 2

Cucumber
x 1 (200 g)

Basil
1 bunch

Soy sauce
4 tablespoons

Oranges
x 4

  **Salt, pepper**

Preparation: 15 minutes

• Squeeze the **oranges**. Cut the **cucumber** and **tomatoes** into small cubes. Pick the **basil** leaves and chop.
• Mix all the ingredients with the **orange juice** and **soy sauce**. Season with salt and pepper and serve.

AÏOLI

42 kcal/person

To serve with:
Steamed or boiled vegetables
Grilled meat, fish or poultry
Steamed fish, shellfish or poultry
Wholemeal pasta
Brown rice
Jacket potatoes

Garlic
15 cloves

Powdered saffron
1 g

Low-fat cream cheese
120 g

 **Salt, pepper**

Preparation: 15 minutes
Cooking: 30 minutes

• Peel the **garlic** cloves and remove the green germs. Cook in 200 ml water for about 30 minutes over low heat or until tender enough to be crushed with a fork. Take off the heat and leave to cool.

• Add the saffron and the **cream cheese** to the crushed garlic. Purée with a hand blender. Season with salt and pepper and serve.

RED WINE SAUCE

108 kcal/person

To serve with:
Grilled meat, fish or poultry
Poached or boiled eggs
Steamed vegetables
Seafood
Fried Brussels sprouts
Tofu

Shallots
x 6

Red wine
500 ml

Garlic
2 cloves

Bouquets garnis
x 2

Beef stock
300 ml

 Salt, pepper

Preparation: 15 minutes
Cooking: 1 hour

• Peel the **shallots** and **garlic**, slice thinly and place in a saucepan with the **red wine**, **stock** and **bouquets garnis**.

• Cook over low heat for about 1 hour until the sauce is reduced by a quarter and thickens. Season with salt and pepper and serve hot.

RAVIGOTE SAUCE

109 kcal/person

To serve with:

Artichoke bottoms
Tinned salsify
Poached chicken
Steamed quenelles
Lettuce or chicory hearts
Roasts
Tomato salad
Meat
Grilled fish

Strong mustard
1 tablespoon

Eggs
2 (hardboiled)

Parsley
1 bunch

Low-fat cream cheese
180 g

Cornichons
x 16

Preparation: 15 minutes

• Pick the **parsley** leaves and chop. Mix with the **cream cheese**, chopped **cornichons**, crushed hardboiled **eggs** and **mustard**.

178

BOLOGNESE SAUCE

123 kcal/person

—

To serve with:
Steamed vegetables
Palm hearts
Wholemeal pasta
Green cabbage
Cauliflower
Brussels sprouts
Courgette rounds

Tomatoes
500 g (ripe)

Turkey escalopes
x 2 (150 g each)

Sweet onion
x 1

Tomato purée
2 tablespoons

Dried thyme
1 tablespoon

 Salt, pepper

Preparation: 15 minutes
Cooking: 45 minutes

• Cut the **turkey escalopes** into cubes and the **tomatoes** and **onion** into small pieces. Cook with the **tomato purée** and **thyme** in 200 ml water for 45 minutes over low heat.
• Purée with a hand blender. Season with salt and pepper and serve.

CARBONARA SAUCE

152 kcal/person

—

To serve with:
Steamed vegetables
Palm hearts
Wholemeal pasta
Brussels sprouts
Courgette rounds

Eggs
x 2 (yolks)

Feta
50 g

Cooked ham
2 slices

Grated nutmeg
¼ tablespoon

Low-fat cream cheese
120 g

 **Salt, pepper**

👤👤👤👤

Preparation: 10 minutes

• In a salad bowl, mix together the **cream cheese**, **egg** yolks, crushed **feta**, the **ham**, cut into small pieces, and the grated **nutmeg**.
• Season with salt and pepper and mix with cooked vegetables or pasta just before serving.

VINAIGRETTE

20 kcal/person

To serve with:

Salads

Steamed fish, shellfish or poultry

Steamed or boiled vegetables

White beans

Lentils

Semolina

Orange
x 1

Wholegrain mustard
2 tablespoons

Soy sauce
4 tablespoons

 **Salt, pepper**

👤👤👤👤

⏱

Preparation: 5 minutes

• Squeeze the **orange**. Mix the juice with the **mustard**, **soy sauce** and 6 tablespoons of water. Season with salt and pepper and serve.

184

CURRY SAUCE

258 kcal/person

To serve with:
Steamed poultry or fish
Grilled or steamed seafood
Steamed vegetables
Vegetable sticks
Grilled meat or fish
Baked pumpkin
Wholemeal pasta
Brown rice

Curry powder
2 tablespoons

Mango
x ½

Apple
x 1

Coconut milk
400 ml

Coriander
20 leaves

  **Salt, pepper**

Preparation: 15 minutes
Cooking: 30 minutes

• Peel the **mango** and **apple** and cut into small pieces. Cook in a casserole with the **coconut milk** and the **curry powder** for 30 minutes over very low heat.

• Purée with a hand blender. Season with salt and pepper, add the chopped **coriander** and serve.

BARBECUE SAUCE

86 kcal/person

To serve with:

Meat

Fish

Grilled poultry

Grilled or steamed fish or shellfish

Roasts

Skewers of meat or fish

Grilled vegetables

Grilled or steamed sausages

Tofu

Red kidney beans
1 small tin

Tomato purée
1 tablespoon

Apple
x 1

Liquid honey
3 tablespoons

Soy sauce
6 tablespoons

Preparation: 15 minutes
Cooking: 30 minutes

• Peel the **apple** and cut into small pieces. Cook in a casserole with the drained **red kidney beans**, **tomato purée**, **soy sauce**, **honey** and 20 ml water for 30 minutes over very low heat. Purée with a hand blender and serve.

TOMATO KETCHUP

61 kcal/person

To serve with:

Wholemeal pasta
Brown rice
Grilled meat, fish or poultry
Steamed fish and shellfish
Steamed vegetables
Vegetable sticks
Grated fennel
Omelettes

Tomatoes
500 g

Sweet onion
x 1

Liquid honey
3 tablespoons

Tomato purée
1 tablespoon

Vinegar
2 tablespoons

 Salt, pepper

Preparation: 15 minutes
Cooking: 30 minutes

• De-seed and dice the **tomatoes**. Cook in a saucepan for 30 minutes over low heat with the **tomato purée**, **vinegar**, chopped **onion**, **honey** and 20 ml water until reduced and thick.
• Purée with a hand blender. Season with salt and pepper and serve.

MUSTARD SAUCE

50 kcal/person

—

To serve with:
Grilled meat, fish or poultry
Steamed quenelles
Grilled or poached sausages
Spit-roasted chicken or rabbit
Kidneys
Fried poultry liver
Fried Brussels sprouts
Steamed vegetables
Roasts

Wholegrain mustard
2 tablespoons

Mustard
1 tablespoon

Low-fat cream cheese
120 g

Dried thyme
2 teaspoons

 Salt, pepper

Preparation: 5 minutes
Cooking: 10 minutes

• Mix the ingredients together in a saucepan. Cook for 10 minutes over low heat, beating continuously. Season and serve.

BEEF TARTARE WITH AUBERGINE

313 kcal/person

—

Gluten free

—

Lactose free

Fillet of beef
600 g

Aubergines
x 3 (medium)

Basil
1 bunch

Olive oil
2 tablespoons

 Salt, pepper

👤👤👤👤

🕐
Preparation: 10 minutes
Cooking: 40 minutes

• Chop the **basil**. Cut the **beef** into small, even cubes.

• Cook the **aubergines** whole for 40 minutes in a steamer and leave to cool. Scoop out the flesh with a spoon and mix with the **beef**, **basil** and **olive oil**. Season with salt and pepper and serve.

BEEF TARTARE WITH HERBS

229 kcal/person

—

Gluten free

—

Lactose free

Fillet of beef
400 g

Basil
1 bunch

Coriander
1 bunch

Radishes
x 12

Sesame seeds
2 tablespoons

 **Salt, pepper**

2 tablespoons sesame oil

Preparation: 20 minutes

• Trim and dice the **radishes**. Chop the **herbs**.
• Cut the **beef** into small pieces.
• Mix all the ingredients in a salad bowl, add 2 tablespoons sesame oil, season with salt and pepper and serve.

STEAMED RIB OF BEEF

586 kcal/person

—

Steam

—

Gluten free

Rib of beef
x 1 (not too fatty)

Egg
x 1

Tarragon
1 bunch

Mustard
1 teaspoon

Low-fat cream cheese
120 g

 Salt, pepper

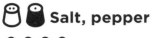

Preparation: 15 minutes
Cooking: 15 minutes

• Separate the **egg**. Beat the yolk with the **mustard**, the **cream cheese** and the chopped **tarragon**.

• Beat the egg-white until stiff and fold into the cream cheese mixture.

• Cook the **rib of beef** for exactly 15 minutes in a steamer. Cut into slices, season with salt and pepper and serve with the sauce.

PORK SKEWERS WITH APRICOT

135 kcal/person

—

Steam

—

Lactose free

Pork fillet
x 1

Apricots
x 8

Soy sauce
2 tablespoons

Liquid honey
1 tablespoon

Coriander
x 4 sprigs

Preparation: 15 minutes
Cooking: 20 minutes

• Cut the **pork** and **apricots** into even-sized pieces. Assemble 8 skewers with alternate pieces of meat and fruit.
• Cook the skewers for 20 minutes in a steamer. Arrange in a serving dish and pour over the **soy sauce** and **honey**. Serve with the **coriander** sprigs.

BLANQUETTE OF VEAL WITH COCONUT MILK

747 kcal/person

—

Gluten free

—

Lactose free

Stewing veal
1.2 kg

Garden peas
100 g

Mange-tout
100 g

Baby spinach
100 g

Coconut milk
400 ml

 Salt, pepper

🕐

Preparation: 20 minutes
Cooking:
1 hour 10 minutes

• Cook the **veal** in a casserole with 1 litre of water for 1 hour over low heat. Remove the **veal** and set aside. Add the **coconut milk** to the casserole and reduce to half. Add the **mange-tout**, **garden peas** and the trimmed **spinach**.

• Cook for a further 10 minutes over low heat, return the meat to the casserole, season with salt and pepper and serve.

PORK FILLET WITH LEEK

135 kcal/person

—

Steam

—

Lactose free

Pork fillet
x 1 (without fat)

Leek
x 1

Wholegrain mustard
3 tablespoons

 Salt, pepper

Preparation: 15 minutes
Cooking: 43 minutes

• Cut the **leek** in half lengthways. Wash under cold running water and plunge into boiling water for 3 minutes.

• Brush the **pork fillet** with **mustard**, then wrap the **leek** leaves around it. Cook for 40 minutes in a steamer. Season with salt and pepper.

• Cut into thick slices and serve with salad and mustard sauce (see page 192).

VEAL WITH CARROTS AND ROSEMARY

567 kcal/person

—

Gluten free

—

Lactose free

Stewing veal
1.2 kg

Carrots
x 8

Rosemary
3 sprigs

Sweet onions
x 2

 Salt, pepper

🕐
Preparation: 10 minutes
Cooking: 1 hour
30 minutes

• Place the **veal**, the **rosemary** sprigs cut in half, the sliced **carrots** and the chopped **onion** in a casserole.
• Just cover with water and cook with the lid on for 1 hour 30 minutes over very low heat. Season and serve straight from the casserole.

206

PORK, CHANTERELLES AND BLUEBERRIES

140 kcal/person

—

Lactose free

Pork fillet
x 1 (without fat)

Chanterelles
300 g

Blueberries
x 32

Soy sauce
4 tablespoons

 Salt, pepper

Preparation: 15 minutes
Cooking: 5 minutes

• Cut the **pork fillet** into cubes. Rinse and dry the **chanterelles**.

• Seal the meat for 1 minute in a very hot, dry, non-stick pan. Season with salt and pepper and cook for a further 1 minute.

• Add the **chanterelles**, **blueberries** and **soy sauce**, cook for a further 3 minutes and serve.

CHICKEN WITH PEPPERS AND BASIL

348 kcal/person

—

Gluten free

—

Lactose free

Chicken breasts
x 4

Red peppers
x 2

Garlic
6 cloves

Basil
1 bunch

White onion
x 1

 Salt, pepper

Preparation: 10 minutes
Cooking: 50 minutes

- Cut the **peppers** into pieces and cook in a casserole with the peeled **garlic** and chopped **onion** in 200 ml water for 30 minutes over low heat.
- Purée with a hand blender.
- Add the **chicken**, cut into rough cubes, season with salt and pepper and cook for a further 20 minutes. Take off the heat, add the chopped **basil** and serve.

STEAMED FILLET STEAK

360 kcal/person

—

Steam

—

Gluten free

Fillet steaks
x 4 (170 g each)

Wholegrain mustard
4 tablespoons

Dill
2 bunches

Low-fat cream cheese
240 g

Raspberry vinegar
2 tablespoons

 Salt, pepper

Preparation: 10 minutes
Cooking: 5 minutes

• Mix together the **cream cheese**, **mustard**, **vinegar** and three-quarters of the chopped **dill**.

• Season the steaks with salt and pepper. Cook for 5 minutes in a steamer.

• Slice the meat and arrange in a serving dish, sprinkle with the remaining **dill** and serve with the sauce.

CHICKEN AND PUMPKIN SKEWERS

278 kcal/person

—

Gluten free

—

Lactose free

Pumpkin
200 g

Chicken breasts
600 g

Sesame seeds
2 tablespoons

Balsamic vinegar
2 tablespoons

Mange-tout
x 32

 Salt, pepper

Preparation: 20 minutes
Cooking: 25 minutes

• Pre-heat the oven to 180°C.
• Trim the **mange-tout**. Cut the **pumpkin** and **chicken** into pieces and assemble 4 skewers, alternating the **pumpkin**, **chicken** and **mange-tout**.
• Arrange the skewers in an ovenproof dish. Season with salt and pepper, sprinkle with the **vinegar** and bake in the oven for 25 minutes. Sprinkle with **sesame seeds** and serve.

TOMATO BURGER

269 kcal/person

—

Gluten free

—

Lactose free

Tomatoes
x 4 (large)

Beefburgers
x 4 (100 g each)

Mustard
1 teaspoon

Lettuce
8 leaves

Cooked ham
2 slices

 **Salt, pepper**

1 drizzle olive oil

Preparation: 15 minutes
Cooking: 7 minutes

• Seal the **beefburgers** for 1 minute on each side in a pan with a drizzle of olive oil.
• Cut the **tomatoes** in half and brush the insides with **mustard**. Place half a slice of **ham** on one half, a **beefburger** on the other and cook in the oven for 5 minutes at 180°C.
• Add the **lettuce** leaves and assemble the burgers. Season with salt and pepper and serve.

PARSNIPS AND CHICKEN LIVERS WITH PORT

228 kcal/person

—

Gluten free

Chicken livers
x 8

Parsnips
x 4

Ruby port
4 tablespoons

Blueberries
x 20

Fromage frais
2 tablespoons

Salt, pepper

1 drizzle olive oil

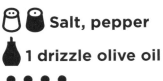

Preparation: 15 minutes
Cooking: 27 minutes

• Peel the **parsnips** and cook for 25 minutes in just enough water to cover. Purée with a hand blender. Add the **fromage frais** and season with salt and pepper.

• Seal the **livers** for 1 minute on each side in a frying pan with a drizzle of olive oil. Add the **port** and **blueberries**. Reduce, stirring continuously. Arrange the livers on the **parsnip** purée and serve.

TURKEY ESCALOPES WITH MUSHROOMS

213 kcal/person

Turkey escalopes
x 4

Closed-cup mushrooms
500 g

Tarragon
1 bunch

Low-fat cream
500 ml

Soy sauce
4 tablespoons

Salt, pepper

1 drizzle olive oil

Preparation: 20 minutes
Cooking: 22 minutes

• Seal the **turkey escalope** for 1 minute on each side in a frying pan with a drizzle of olive oil. Add the **soy sauce**, sliced **mushrooms** and **cream**.
• Cook for 20 minutes over low heat, stirring continuously. Season with salt and pepper. Add the chopped **tarragon**, mix and serve.

POACHED CHICKEN WITH GINGER AND LEMON GRASS

477 kcal/person

—

Gluten free

—

Lactose free

Chicken
x 1

Fresh ginger
100 g

Lemon grass
4 stems

White onions
x 2

Thyme
5 sprigs

 Salt, pepper

✘✘✘✘

🕐

Preparation: 10 minutes
Cooking: 1 hour

• Place the **chicken** in a casserole with the peeled and sliced **ginger**, **lemon grass**, cut into pieces, thinly sliced **onions** and **thyme**.
• Cover with water, season with salt and pepper and simmer for 1 hour over low heat.
• Cut the **chicken** into pieces and serve the bouillon separately.

PEAS AND DUCK WITH SAGE

405 kcal/person

—

Gluten free

—

Lactose free

Strips of duck
x 8

Sage leaves
x 8

Peas
500 g (fresh or frozen)

Olive oil
2 tablespoons

 **Salt, pepper**

Preparation: 15 minutes
Cooking: 12 minutes

• Heat the **oil** in a frying pan and seal the **duck**. Brown lightly for 1 minute on each side.
• Add the **peas** and the chopped **sage**. Reduce the heat and cook for 10 minutes over low heat, stirring continuously. Season with salt and pepper and serve.

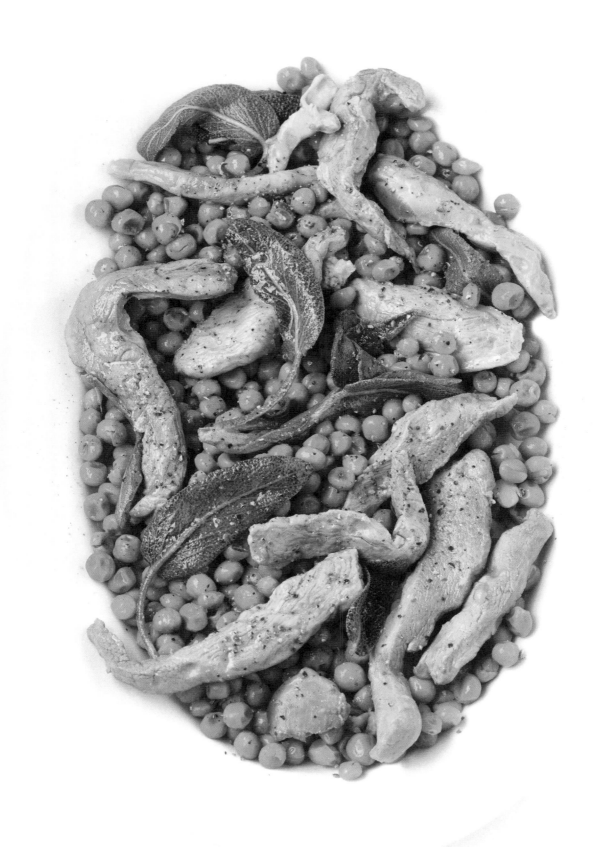

STEAMED VENISON FILLET

169 kcal/person

—

Lactose free

Venison fillet
500 g

Mixed berries
100 g

Soy sauce
6 tablespoons

Tarragon
1 bunch

Pink peppercorns
1 teaspoon

 **Salt, pepper**

Preparation: 10 minutes
Cooking: 6 minutes

• In a saucepan, mix together the **mixed berries**, **soy sauce** and chopped **tarragon**. Cook for 1 minute and set aside.

• Season the **venison** with salt and pepper. Cook for 5 minutes in a steamer. Cut into slices and arrange in a serving dish.

• Sprinkle the meat with crushed **pink peppercorns** and serve with the **berry sauce**.

CHICKEN PARCELS WITH GIROLLES

342 kcal/person

—

Gluten free

Chicken breasts
600 g

Girolles
240 g

Fresh goats' cheese
150 g

Thyme
8 sprigs

 Salt, pepper

1 drizzle walnut oil

Preparation: 15 minutes
Cooking: 25 minutes

• Wash and dry the **girolles**. Pre-heat the oven to 180°C
• Arrange the **cheese**, the **chicken**, cut into pieces, the **girolles** and the **thyme** on 4 sheets of baking paper. Close the parcels tightly and bake in the oven for 25 minutes.
• Arrange the parcels on plates, season with salt and pepper and serve with a drizzle of walnut oil.

TOMATOES STUFFED WITH BEEF AND AUBERGINE

168 kcal/person

—

Gluten free

—

Lactose free

Tomatoes
x 8 (medium)

Aubergines
x 2

Minced beef
200 g

Dried thyme
2 tablespoons

 Salt, pepper

Preparation: 20 minutes
Cooking: 1 hour

• Cook the **aubergines** for 40 minutes in a steamer. Scoop out the flesh and mix with the **beef** and **thyme**. Season with salt and pepper.
• Pre-heat the oven to 180°C.
• Hollow out the **tomatoes** and stuff them with the beef and aubergine mixture. Arrange the stuffed **tomatoes** in an oven dish, add the scooped out **tomato** flesh to the dish and bake for 20 minutes. Serve very hot.

PEAS WITH MERGUEZ SAUSAGE AND BROCCOLI

194 kcal/person

—

Gluten free

—

Lactose free

Peas
400 g

Merguez sausage
x 2

Cherry tomatoes
200 g

Broccoli
250 g

Dried oregano
1 tablespoon

 **Salt, pepper**

Preparation: 15 minutes
Cooking: 42 minutes

• Prick the **sausages** and boil for 20 minutes. Cut into pieces and seal for 1 minute on each side in a dry frying pan.

• Add the **peas**, the halved **cherry tomatoes**, the **broccoli**, cut into pieces, and the **oregano**. Cook for 20 minutes, stirring continuously. Season with salt and pepper and serve.

LOW-FAT STEW

544 kcal/person

—

Gluten free

—

Lactose free

Chuck steak
900 g

Turnips
x 4

Carrots
x 4

Fennel
2 bulbs

Bouquet garni
x 1

 **Salt, pepper**

👤👤👤👤

🕐
Preparation: 10 minutes
Cooking: 2 hours

• Place the **steak** in a casserole and just cover with water. Bring to the boil, then pour off the water and rinse the meat.

• Return the meat to the casserole, add the peeled **turnips**, **carrots** and **fennel**, the **bouquet garni** and 2 litres of water, cover and cook for 2 hours over low heat. Season with salt and pepper and serve straight from the casserole.

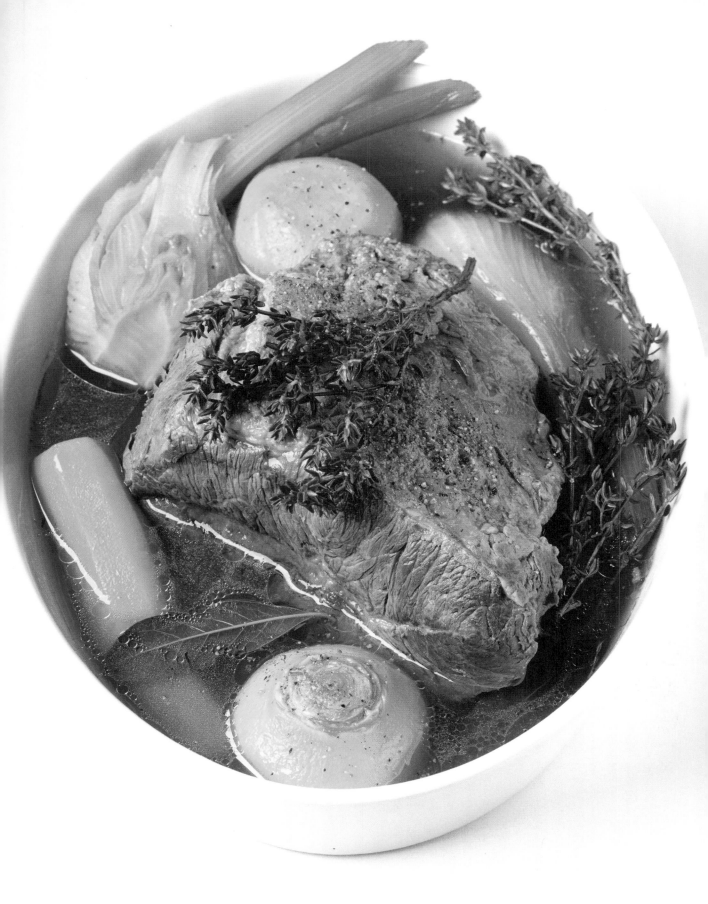

PAN-FRIED BEEF WITH CARROTS

299 kcal/person

—

Gluten free

—

Lactose free

Steaks
x 4 (about 600 g)

Carrots
500 g

Flat-leaf parsley
4 sprigs

Olive oil
2 tablespoons

 Salt, pepper

Preparation: **20 minutes**
Cooking: **3 minutes**

• Peel and grate the **carrots**. Cut the **steaks** into small pieces. Chop the **parsley**.

• Heat the **oil** in a frying pan and seal the pieces of meat. Fry for 1 minute over high heat, then add the **carrots** and **parsley**. Season with salt and pepper, cook for a further 2 minutes, stirring continuously, and serve.

TURKEY ESCALOPES WITH TOMATO

202 kcal/person

—

Gluten free

—

Lactose free

Turkey escalopes
x 4 (fairly thin)

Tomatoes
x 3 (large)

Bouquets garnis
x 2

White wine
80 ml

 **Salt, pepper**

Preparation: 10 minutes
Cooking: 45 minutes

• Pre-heat the oven to 180°C. Cut the **turkey escalopes** in half.

• Cut the **tomatoes** into thick slices and arrange in a gratin dish, interspersed with the meat.

• Add the **white wine** and **bouquets garnis**. Season with salt and pepper and bake in the oven for 45 minutes, basting occasionally.

BLANQUETTE OF VEAL WITH PUMPKIN

542 kcal/person

—

Gluten free

—

Lactose free

Stewing veal
1.2 kg

Pumpkin
500 g

White onions
x 2

Sesame seeds
2 teaspoons

Coriander
4 sprigs

 Salt, pepper

1 tablespoon sesame oil

Preparation: 20 minutes
Cooking:
1 hour 30 minutes

• In a casserole cook the **veal** and the thinly sliced **onions** in 1.5 litres of water for 1 hour over very low heat. Drain the meat on a plate.

• Add the **pumpkin**, peeled and cut into pieces, to the casserole and cook for 30 minutes. Purée with a hand blender. Season with salt and pepper.

• Return the meat to the casserole and add the **coriander** and the **sesame seeds** and oil.

TURKEY, PUMPKIN AND SAGE PARCELS

265 kcal/person

—

Gluten free

—

Lactose free

Turkey escalopes
x 4

Pumpkin
400 g

Paprika
1 tablespoon

Sage
12 leaves

Walnut oil
2 tablespoons

 Salt, pepper

Preparation: 15 minutes
Cooking: 35 minutes

• Pre-heat the oven to 180°C. Peel and cut the **pumpkin** and the **turkey escalopes** into equal-sized pieces.

• Arrange the **pumpkin** and **turkey** pieces with the **sage** and **paprika** on 4 sheets of baking paper. Season and close the parcels tightly. Bake for 35 minutes. Transfer to plates and serve with the walnut oil drizzled over.

RABBIT IN WHITE WINE SAUCE WITH MUSHROOMS

407 kcal/person

—

Gluten free

—

Lactose free

Rabbit legs
x 4

Closed-cup mushrooms
500 g

Carrots
x 4 (large)

White wine
500 ml

Bouquets garnis
x 2

 **Salt, pepper**

👤👤👤👤

🕐
Preparation: 15 minutes
Cooking: 1 hour
30 minutes

• Place the **rabbit legs**, the **mushrooms**, cut into quarters, the peeled and sliced **carrots** and the **bouquets garnis** in a casserole.

• Add the **white wine** and 300 ml water, cover and simmer for 1 hour 30 minutes over very low heat. Season with salt and pepper and serve straight from the casserole.

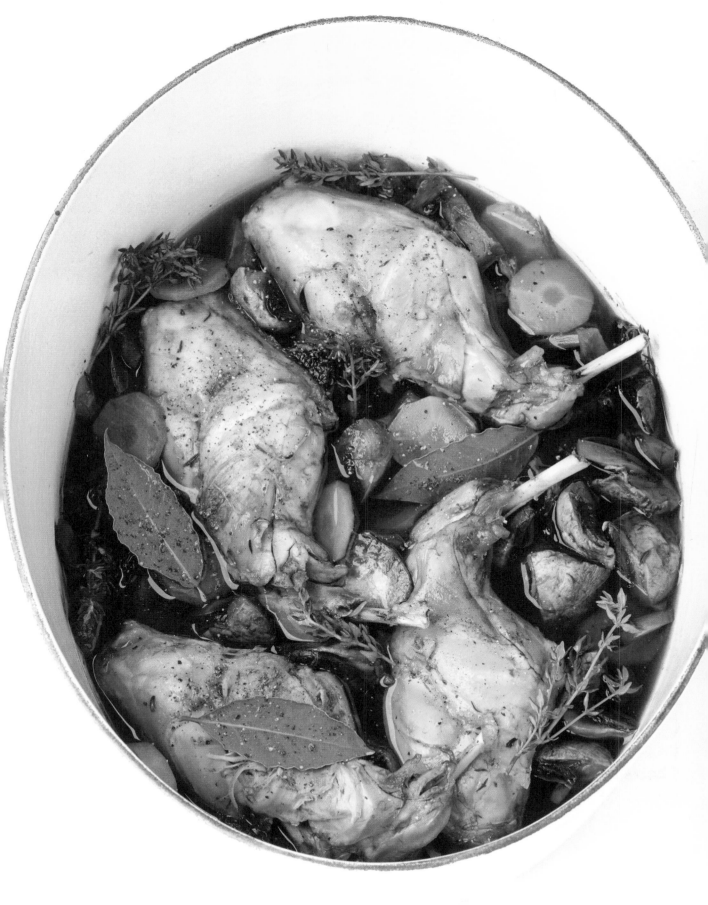

STUFFED AUBERGINES

140 kcal/person

—

Gluten free

Aubergines
x 2

Minced beef
200 g

Cumin seeds
2 teaspoons

Coriander
12 sprigs

Fromage frais
4 tablespoons

 **Salt, pepper**

Preparation: 20 minutes
Cooking: 1 hour

• Cook the **aubergines** whole for 40 minutes in a steamer. Scoop out the flesh with a spoon and mix with the **beef**, **fromage frais**, **cumin** and chopped **coriander**. Season with salt and pepper.
• Pre-heat the oven to 180°C.
• Stuff the **aubergines** with the meat mixture and bake in the oven for 20 minutes. Serve hot.

LAMB STEW

581 kcal/person

—

Gluten free

—

Lactose free

Lamb leg, chump off
x 1 (about 1.2 kg)

Baby turnips
1 bunch

Baby carrots
1 bunch

Bouquets garnis
x 2

Leek
x 1

 **Salt, pepper**

Preparation: 20 minutes
Cooking: 2 hours

• Remove the fat from the **lamb** and cook for 1 hour in a large casserole with the **bouquets garnis** in 3 litres of water.

• Add the washed and chopped leek, the peeled turnips and carrots and cook for a further 1 hour over low heat. Season with salt and pepper and serve straight from the casserole.

STEAMED MEATBALLS WITH BASIL

321 kcal/person

—

Steam

—

Lactose free

Minced beef
500 g

Cumin seeds
1 tablespoon

Basil
1 bunch

Anise seeds
1 tablespoon

 **Salt, pepper**

1 drizzle olive oil

Preparation: 20 minutes
Cooking: 3 minutes

• Chop the **basil**. Mix the **beef** with the spices and chopped **basil**. Season with salt and pepper.
• Shape into 8 equal-sized meatballs and cook for 3 minutes in a steamer.
• Serve the meatballs with a drizzle of olive oil.

QUINOA WITH CHICKEN

530 kcal/person

—

Steam

—

Gluten free

Chicken legs
x 4

Merguez sausages
x 2

Courgettes
x 2

Carrots
x 4

Quinoa
250 g

 Salt, pepper

Preparation: 15 minutes
Cooking: 35 minutes

• Remove the skin from the **chicken legs** and cook them for 35 minutes in a steamer with the **sausages**, the **courgettes**, cut into thick rounds, and the peeled **carrots**.

• Cook the **quinoa** in 1 litre of water. Spread out in a serving dish and add the meat and vegetables. Season with salt and pepper and serve with fresh coriander or cumin seeds, if liked.

STEAMED FILLET STEAK WITH TARRAGON

332 kcal/person

—

Steam

—

Gluten free

Steaks
x 4 (170 g each)

Tarragon
2 bunches

Fromage frais
80 g

  **Salt, pepper**

Preparation: 5 minutes
Cooking: 5 minutes

• Mix half the chopped **tarragon** with the **fromage frais**.
• 10 minutes before serving, cook the **steaks** for exactly 5 minutes in a steamer. Leave to rest for 30 seconds.
• Spread the tarragon mixture over the base of a serving dish and arrange the sliced meat on top. Sprinkle with the remaining **tarragon** and season with salt and pepper.

ROAST CHICKEN LEGS WITH MUSTARD

294 kcal/person

—

Gluten free

Chicken legs
x 4

Mustard
4 tablespoons

Thyme
4 sprigs

Low-fat cream cheese
180 g

Preparation: 10 minutes
Cooking: 40 minutes

• Pre-heat the oven to 180°C. Mix the **cream cheese** with the **mustard** and **thyme**. Season with salt and pepper.

• Remove the skin from the **chicken legs** and brush them with the mustard mixture. Place in an ovenproof dish, bake for 40 minutes and serve.

SALMON, AVOCADO AND MUSHROOMS

477 kcal/person

—

Gluten free

—

Lactose free

Salmon steaks
x 4 (with skin)

Avocado
x 1

Closed-cup mushrooms
x 8 (large)

Chives
1 bunch

Lime
x 1

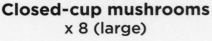 Salt, pepper

Preparation: 15 minutes
Cooking: 20 minutes

• Pre-heat the oven to 180°C. Cook the **salmon steaks** skin side down for 20 minutes.

• Peel and slice the **avocado**. Cut up the **chives** and slice the **mushrooms** thinly. Mix with the juice of the **lime**. Serve the salmon hot, covered with the avocado and mushroom mixture. Season with salt and pepper and serve.

POACHED SCALLOPS WITH SAFFRON

58 kcal/person

—

Gluten free

—

Lactose free

Scallops
x 12 (with or without coral)

Green asparagus
x 8

Cherry tomatoes
x 8

Saffron
5 threads

 **Salt, pepper**

Preparation: 15 minutes
Cooking: 5 minutes

• Trim the **asparagus** and cut into pieces. Cut the **tomatoes** in half.
• Place all the ingredients in a casserole with 500 ml water and cook for 5 minutes over very low heat. Season with salt and pepper, leave to stand for 5 minutes and serve.

BAKED BASS WITH A VITAMIN-RICH SAUCE

273 kcal/person

—

Lactose free

Whole bass
x 1 (1 kg, scaled and gutted)

Coriander
1 bunch

Passion fruit
x 2

Kiwis
x 2

Soy sauce
4 tablespoons

 Salt, pepper

Preparation: 10 minutes
Cooking: 25 minutes

• Pre-heat the oven to 180°C. Peel and dice the **kiwis**. Scoop out the pulp of the **passion fruit** and mix with the **kiwis**, **soy sauce** and the chopped **coriander**.

• Bake the **bass** whole for 25 minutes. Prick to test if it is cooked. Season with salt and pepper and serve with the sauce. Garnish with lemon slices and thyme sprigs, if liked.

COD WITH HERBS

168 kcal/person

—

Lactose free

Cod loin
800 g

Mandarins
x 3

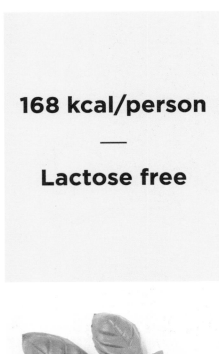

Basil
1 bunch

Coriander
1 bunch

Soy sauce
4 tablespoons

 1 drizzle olive oil

🕐

Preparation: 15 minutes
Cooking: 10 minutes

• Pre-heat the oven to 180°C. Roughly chop the herbs. Squeeze the **mandarins** and strain the juice.

• Put the **cod** in an ovenproof dish and bake for 10 minutes. Pour over the **mandarin** juice and **soy sauce**. Sprinkle with the herbs and serve with a drizzle of olive oil.

CHINESE-STYLE SEA BREAM

210 kcal/person

—

Lactose free

Red sea bream
x 1 (scaled and gutted)

Leek
x 1 (small)

Fresh ginger
150 g

Lemon grass
2 stems

Soy sauce
4 tablespoons

Preparation: 20 minutes
Cooking: 30 minutes

• Pre-heat the oven to 180°C. Peel and grate the **ginger** with a hand grater. Wash and cut the **leek** and the **lemon grass** into very thin strips.

• Place the **sea bream** in an ovenproof dish. Add the other ingredients and a glass of water, then bake in the oven for 30 minutes, basting regularly with the cooking juices. Serve with the **soy sauce** drizzled over. Garnish with coriander leaves, if liked.

OCTOPUS WITH HERBS

180 kcal/person

—

Gluten free

—

Lactose free

Octopus
x 1 (about 1 kg)

Cherry tomatoes
650 g

White wine
50 ml

Bouquet garni
x 1

Capers
100 g

 Salt, pepper

Preparation: 15 minutes
Cooking: 40 minutes

• Place the **octopus** in a casserole. Cover with water and bring to the boil. Cook for 20 minutes, then take off the heat and leave the **octopus** to cool in the casserole.

• Cook the halved **tomatoes** for 20 minutes with the **white wine**, 50 ml of the cooking water, the **capers** and the **bouquet garni**. Add the **octopus**, cut into pieces. Season and serve.

SAUERKRAUT WITH PRAWNS AND CUMIN

365 kcal/person

—

Lactose free

Uncooked giant prawns
x 4 (peeled)

Cooked sauerkraut
500 g

Cumin seeds
2 tablespoons

Dill
1 bunch

Beer
200 ml

 **Salt, pepper**

👤👤👤👤

🕐

Preparation: 5 minutes
Cooking: 20 minutes

• In a casserole, cook the **sauerkraut** with the **beer** and **cumin** for 20 minutes over low heat. Half-way through the cooking time, add the halved **prawns**. Season with salt and pepper.
• Transfer the **prawn sauerkraut** to a serving dish, sprinkle with chopped **dill** and serve.

MACKEREL PARCELS

240 kcal/person

—

Gluten free

—

Lactose free

Mackerel
4 fillets

Wholegrain mustard
2 tablespoons

Leek
x 1 (small)

Rosemary
4 sprigs

Preparation: 15 minutes
Cooking: 20 minutes

• Pre-heat the oven to 180°C. Arrange the washed and thinly sliced leek, the **mackerel**, **rosemary** and **mustard** on 4 sheets of baking paper.
• Close the parcels tightly and bake in the oven for 20 minutes. Transfer to plates and serve.

CLAMS MARINIÈRE WITH HAM

270 kcal/person
—
Gluten free

Clams
x 60 (cleaned)

Cooked ham
3 slices (without rind)

Low-fat cream
200 ml

Lemon thyme
1 bunch

Preparation: 20 minutes
Cooking: 10 minutes

• Chop the slices of **ham** very finely. Cook the **clams** over high heat in 20 ml water with the **thyme** until they open.
• Divide the **clams** into 4 bowls. Strain the cooking liquid, add the **cream** and bring to the boil. Pour the cream mixture over the **clams**.
• Add the chopped **ham**, mix gently and serve.

STEAMED SWORDFISH WITH HERBS

237 kcal/person

—

Steam

—

Gluten free

Swordfish
4 slices

Cherry tomatoes
x 8

Dried oregano
2 teaspoons

Olive oil
2 tablespoons

Capers
4 teaspoons

 Salt, pepper

Preparation: 10 minutes
Cooking: 5 minutes

• Cut the **tomatoes** into quarters and mix with the **capers**, **oregano** and **olive oil**. Season with salt and pepper.

• Cook the **swordfish** slices for 5 minutes in a steamer. Transfer to a serving dish, pour over the tomato and herb mixture and serve.

COLEY PARCELS WITH LEMON

150 kcal/person

—

Gluten free

—

Lactose free

Coley
4 fillets

Black olives
x 20 (stoned)

Lemons
x 2

Tomatoes
x 4 (medium)

Rosemary
4 sprigs

 **Salt, pepper**

Preparation: 10 minutes
Cooking: 15 minutes

• Pre-heat the oven to 180°C.
• Arrange the **coley**, sliced **tomatoes** and **lemons**, **rosemary** and **olives** on 4 sheets of baking paper.
• Close the parcels tightly. Bake in the oven for 15 minutes. Transfer to plates, season and serve.

COLEY WITH MUSHROOMS

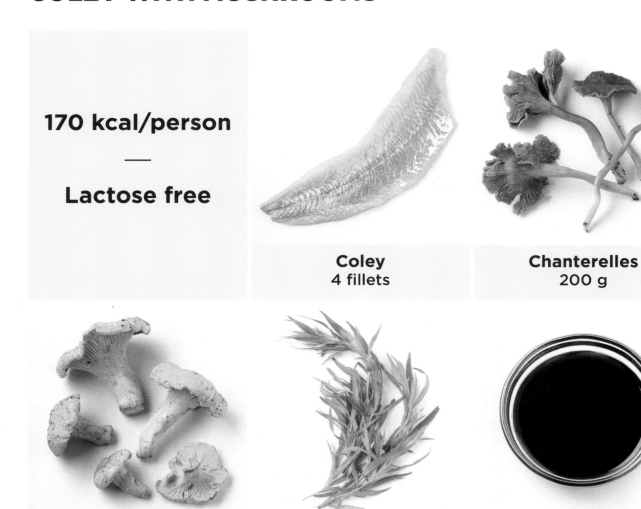

170 kcal/person

—

Lactose free

Coley
4 fillets

Chanterelles
200 g

Girolles
200 g

Tarragon
1 bunch

Soy sauce
8 tablespoons

Preparation: 10 minutes
Cooking: 15 minutes

• Pre-heat the oven to 180°C. Place the **coley** in a large ovenproof dish, add the washed and chopped **mushrooms**, 20 ml water and the **soy sauce**. Bake in the oven for 15 minutes.

• Add the chopped **tarragon** and serve straight from the ovenproof dish.

SALMON PAUPIETTES

410 kcal/person

—

Steam

—

Gluten free

Salmon fillets
400 g (skinless)

Smoked salmon
8 slices

Salmon roe
4 teaspoons

Limes
x 2

 Salt, pepper

Preparation: 15 minutes
Cooking: 3 minutes

• Cut the **salmon fillets** into pieces and mix with the **salmon roe** and the juice of the **limes**. Season with salt and pepper.

• Arrange the mixture in the middle of the slices of **smoked salmon**. Roll up carefully to form small paupiettes.

• Place the paupiettes on baking paper and cook for 3 minutes in a steamer.

TURBOT PARCELS WITH ORANGE

260 kcal/person
—
Lactose free

Turbots
x 2 (700 g each)

Oranges
x 2

Thyme
6 sprigs

Olive oil
1 tablespoon

Soy sauce
4 tablespoons

Preparation: 10 minutes
Cooking: 25 minutes

• Squeeze 1 **orange** and cut the second into slices.
• Arrange the **turbots**, the **orange** slices and juice, the **thyme** and the **olive oil** on 2 large sheets of baking paper.
• Close the parcels tightly. Bake in the oven for 25 minutes and prick to check if they are cooked. Serve with the **soy sauce** drizzled over.

COD PARCELS

120 kcal/person

—

Gluten free

—

Lactose free

Cod loin steaks
600 g

Radishes
x 12

Cucumber
100 g

Anise seeds
2 teaspoons

 Salt, pepper

1 drizzle olive oil

Preparation: 15 minutes
Cooking: 25 minutes

• Pre-heat the oven to 180°C.
• Place the **cod loin steaks** on 4 sheets of baking paper. Add the thinly sliced **radishes** and **cucumber**. Sprinkle with **anise seeds** and season with salt and pepper.
• Close the parcels tightly and bake in the oven for 25 minutes. Serve with a drizzle of olive oil.

SEA BREAM PARCELS WITH THYME

133 kcal/person

—

Gluten free

—

Lactose free

Sea bream
4 fillets

Cherry tomatoes
x 12

Courgettes
x 2 (small)

Thyme
12 sprigs

Bay leaves
x 4

 Salt, pepper

1 drizzle olive oil

Preparation: 20 minutes
Cooking: 25 minutes

• Pre-heat the oven to 180°C.
• Place the **sea bream** on 4 sheets of baking paper. Add the halved **tomatoes**, grated **courgettes**, the **thyme** and the **bay leaves**. Season with salt and pepper.
• Close the parcels tightly and bake in the oven for 25 minutes. Serve with a drizzle of olive oil.

SALMON WITH ASPARAGUS

104 kcal/person

—

Gluten free

—

Lactose free

Salmon steaks
x 4

Green asparagus
x 16

Pumpkin seeds
2 tablespoons

  Salt, pepper

 1 drizzle olive oil

Preparation: 10 minutes
Cooking: 5 minutes

• Trim the **asparagus** and cut into pieces.
• Place the **salmon steaks**, **asparagus** pieces and **pumpkin seeds** in a steamer. Season with salt and pepper and cook for 5 minutes.
• Transfer the **salmon steaks** to plates. Add a drizzle of olive oil and serve.

SCALLOP PARCELS

135 kcal/person

—

Gluten free

—

Lactose free

Scallops
x 12

Uncooked prawns
x 12 (peeled)

Cherry tomatoes
x 24

Dried oregano
1 tablespoon

White wine
4 tablespoons

 **Salt, pepper**

1 drizzle olive oil

Preparation: 10 minutes
Cooking: 25 minutes

- Pre-heat the oven to 180°C.
- Place the **scallops** and **prawns** on 4 sheets of baking paper. Add the **tomatoes**, **white wine** and **oregano**. Season with salt and pepper.
- Close the parcels tightly and bake in the oven for 25 minutes. Serve with a drizzle of olive oil.

MULTI... MULLET WITH ORANGE AND ROSEMARY

200 kcal/person

—

Gluten free

—

Lactose free

Whole mullet
x 4 (scaled and gutted)

Orange
x 1

Rosemary
2 sprigs

Garlic
4 cloves

Limes
x 2

 **Salt, pepper**

1 drizzle olive oil

Preparation: 15 minutes
Cooking: 15 minutes
Marinating: 2 hours

• Place the **mullet** in a large ovenproof dish. Add the **rosemary**, the chopped **garlic** and the juice of the **orange** and **limes**. Season with salt and pepper and marinate for 2 hours in the refrigerator.

• Pre-heat the oven to 180°C and bake the **mullet** in the marinade for 15 minutes. Serve with a drizzle of olive oil.

SCALLOPS WITH CREAMED PARSNIPS

140 kcal/person

—

Gluten free

—

Lactose free

Scallops
x 8 + 4 clean shells

Parsnips
300 g

Unwaxed lemons
x 3

Thyme
4 sprigs

 Salt, pepper

1 drizzle olive oil

Preparation: 20 minutes
Cooking: 35 minutes

• Cook the **parsnips** for 30 minutes in a saucepan with just enough water to cover. Purée with a hand blender.

• Season with salt and pepper and spoon the purée into 4 **scallop** shells. Add the raw **scallops** and the **thyme**. Grate the zest of the **lemons** over the **scallops**. Bake in the oven for 5 minutes at 180°C and serve with a drizzle of olive oil.

OCTOPUS CURRY

594 kcal/person

—

Gluten free

—

Lactose free

Octopus
x 1 (1 kg)

Curry powder
2 tablespoons

Coconut milk
800 ml

Courgettes
x 2

Basil
1 bunch

Preparation: 25 minutes
Cooking: 45 minutes

• Chop the **basil**. Slice the **courgettes** and cook in the **coconut milk** with the **curry powder** for 25 minutes over low heat.

• Place the **octopus** in a casserole, cover with water and bring to the boil. Cook for 20 minutes, then take off the heat and leave to cool in the casserole.

• Cut the **octopus** into pieces and add to the courgette mixture with the basil. Re-heat and serve.

MULLET, CELERIAC AND APPLE

224 kcal/person

—

Gluten free

—

Lactose free

Mullet
8 fillets

Apple
x 1

Celeriac
600 g

Fennel seeds
1 tablespoon

 Salt, pepper

1 drizzle olive oil

Preparation: 20 minutes
Cooking: 45 minutes

• Cut the **apple** (reserving a few slices) and the peeled **celeriac** into cubes. Cook in a saucepan in 500 ml water for 35 minutes over low heat. Purée with a hand blender and season with salt and pepper.

• Pour the purée into a gratin dish. Arrange the **mullet** and the **apple** slices on top, sprinkle with the **fennel seeds** and bake in the oven for 10 minutes. Serve with a drizzle of olive oil.

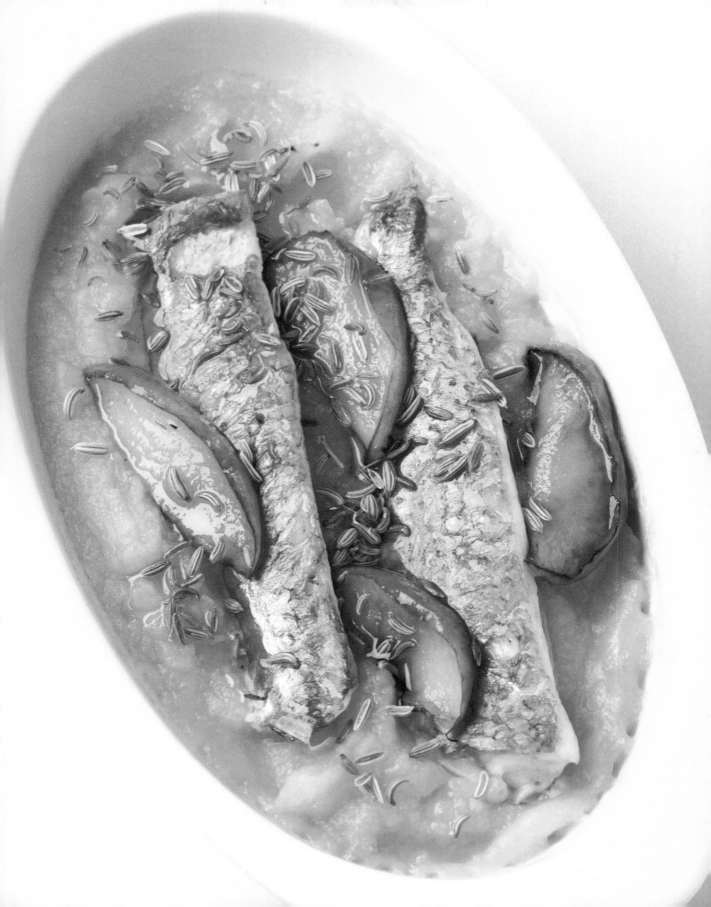

FILLET OF BASS WITH TOMATO

134 kcal/person

—

Steam

—

Gluten free

Bass
4 fillets (skinless)

Tomatoes
x 4 (medium)

Basil
12 large leaves

  Salt, pepper

 1 drizzle olive oil

Preparation: 15 minutes
Cooking: 10 minutes

• Cut the **bass** and **tomatoes** in three. Insert a piece of **bass** and a **basil** leaf between each layer of **tomato**. Season with salt and pepper. Fasten each **tomato** together with a cocktail stick and cook for 10 minutes in a steamer.
• Transfer the **tomatoes** to plates, remove the cocktail sticks and serve with a drizzle of olive oil.

SCALLOPS WITH HONEY AND ASPARAGUS

64 kcal/person

—

Lactose free

Scallops
x 12

Green asparagus
x 12

Liquid honey
2 tablespoons

Thyme
4 sprigs

Soy sauce
3 tablespoons

Salt, pepper

Preparation: 20 minutes
Cooking: 10 minutes

• Trim the **asparagus** and cut into pieces.
• Heat the **honey** in a frying pan. Seal the **scallops** and **asparagus** for 3 minutes on each side in the foaming **honey**. Add the **thyme** and the **soy sauce**.
• Cook for 3 minutes, stirring continuously, season with salt and pepper and serve.

THAI-STYLE SPICED SCALLOPS

130 kcal/person

—

Gluten free

—

Lactose free

Scallops
x 16 (with or without coral)

Fresh ginger
50 g

Red chilli
x 1 (optional)

Lemon grass
2 stems

Basil
20 leaves

Preparation: 10 minutes
Cooking: 15 minutes

• Pre-heat the oven to 180°C. Arrange the
scallops, the peeled and grated **ginger**, the
lemon grass and the finely chopped **chilli**,
if using, on 4 sheets of baking paper.
• Close the parcels tightly and bake in the oven
for 15 minutes. Add the **basil** leaves and serve.

ASIAN-STYLE COD LOIN

367 kcal/person

—

Gluten free

—

Lactose free

Cod loin steaks
x 4 (about 180 g each)

Red peppers
x 2

Preserved lemons
x 2

Coconut milk
400 ml

Black olives
x 20 (stoned)

 **Salt, pepper**

1 drizzle olive oil

Preparation: 25 minutes
Cooking: 40 minutes

• Cut the **peppers** into pieces and cook for 20 minutes in the **coconut milk**. Purée with a hand blender. Season with salt and pepper.
• Pre-heat the oven to 180°C. Place the **cod** in an ovenproof dish and cover with the pepper coulis. Add the **preserved lemons**, cut into pieces, and the olives. Bake in the oven for 20 minutes. Serve with a drizzle of olive oil.

MONKFISH CHEEKS WITH TOMATO

195 kcal/person

—

Gluten free

—

Lactose free

Monkfish cheeks
600 g

Cherry tomatoes
500 g

White wine
100 ml

Basil
20 leaves

Olive oil
1 tablespoon

 Salt, pepper

Preparation: 10 minutes
Cooking: 25 minutes

• In a casserole, cook the **monkfish cheeks** for 25 minutes over low heat with the halved **tomatoes**, **white wine**, 20 ml water and the **olive oil**.

• Season with salt and pepper. Add the **basil** leaves, mix and serve.

STEWED MONKFISH WITH SAFFRON

193 kcal/person

—

Gluten free

—

Lactose free

Monkfish
x 1 (about 800 g)

Leek
x 1

Turnips
x 6

Saffron
10 threads

Carrots
x 4

 **Salt, pepper**

★★★★

Preparation: 15 minutes
Cooking: 45 minutes

• In a casserole, cook the **monkfish**, peeled **carrots**, washed and halved **leek**, peeled and chopped **turnips** and **saffron** in 1.5 litres of water for 45 minutes over very low heat. Add a little water if the bouillon reduces too much. Season with salt and pepper. Serve straight from the casserole.

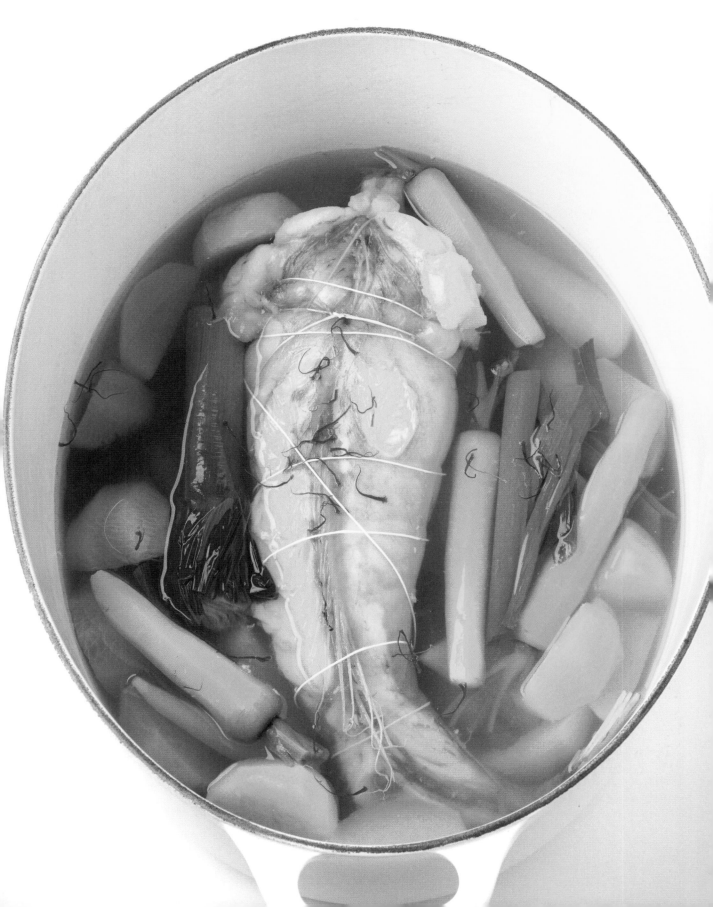

SALMON PARCELS WITH VEGETABLES

322 kcal/person

—

Gluten free

—

Lactose free

Salmon steaks
x 4 (150 g each)

Peas
200 g

Courgette
x 1

Basil
1 bunch

Mange-tout
120 g

 Salt, pepper

1 drizzle olive oil

Preparation: 15 minutes
Cooking: 15 minutes

• Pre-heat the oven to 180°C.
• Arrange the **salmon steaks**, the **courgette**, cut into rounds, and the **peas** and **mange-tout** on 4 sheets of baking paper. Close the parcels tightly.
• Bake in the oven for 15 minutes. Sprinkle with the chopped **basil**, season with salt and pepper and serve with a drizzle of olive oil.

WHITING AND SHELLFISH PARCELS

178 kcal/person

—

Gluten free

—

Lactose free

Whiting
4 fillets

Uncooked prawns
x 8 (peeled)

Cockles
x 20 (cleaned)

Mussels
x 20 (cleaned)

Thyme
8 sprigs

Preparation: 15 minutes
Cooking: 20 minutes

• Pre-heat the oven to 180°C.
• Arrange the **whiting**, **prawns**, **mussels**, **cockles** and **thyme** on 4 sheets of baking paper. Close the parcels tightly.
• Bake in the oven for 20 minutes. Transfer to plates and serve.

JAPANESE-STYLE MACKEREL

304 kcal/person

—

Lactose free

Mackerel
4 fillets (150 g each)

Radishes
x 16

Soy sauce
1 tablespoon

Pickled ginger
30 g

Wasabi
1 teaspoon

Preparation: 15 minutes
Cooking: 20 minutes

• Pre-heat the oven to 180°C.
• Arrange the **mackerel**, the **radishes**, cut into rounds, the **ginger**, **soy sauce** and **wasabi** on 4 sheets of baking paper. Close the parcels tightly.
• Bake in the oven for 20 minutes. Transfer to plates and serve.

MUSSEL PARCELS WITH ROSEMARY

180 kcal/person

—

Gluten free

—

Lactose free

Mussels
2 litres (cleaned)

Rosemary
8 sprigs

Cherry tomatoes
x 20

 Salt, pepper

Preparation: 10 minutes
Cooking: 20 minutes

• Arrange the **mussels**, **rosemary** and the halved **tomatoes** on 4 sheets of baking paper. Close the parcels tightly.

• Bake in the oven for 20 minutes. Season with salt and pepper, transfer to plates and serve.

PEA, GOATS' CHEESE AND SPINACH QUICHE

264 kcal/person

—

Vegetarian

—

Gluten free

Baby spinach
150 g

Eggs
x 4

Fresh goats' cheese
300 g

Tarragon
1 bunch

Peas
400 g

 Salt, pepper

**Preparation: 30 minutes
Cooking: 25 minutes**

• Pre-heat the oven to 200°C. Cover the base of a large tart tin with moistened baking paper.

• Mix together the cheese, **peas**, trimmed **spinach**, chopped **tarragon** and the **eggs**. Season with salt and pepper.

• Pour the mixture into the prepared tin, pressing it down and bake in the oven for 25 minutes. Serve hot or cold.

STUFFED COURGETTE FLOWERS

273 kcal/person

—

Vegetarian

—

Gluten free

Courgette flowers
x 8

Unwaxed lemons
x 2

Dried oregano
2 teaspoons

Egg
x 1

Ricotta
400 g

 Salt, pepper

1 drizzle olive oil

Preparation: 20 minutes
Cooking: 25 minutes

• Pre-heat the oven to 180°C. Mix together the **ricotta**, **oregano**, **egg** and the juice and grated zest of the **lemons**. Season with salt and pepper.
• Trim the **courgettes**. Using a small spoon, carefully fill the flowers with the mixture. Place the **courgette flowers** in an ovenproof dish and bake for 25 minutes. Serve warm or cold with a drizzle of olive oil.

VEGETABLE COUSCOUS

97 kcal/person

—

Steam

—

Vegetarian

Cauliflower
900 g

Baby turnips
1 bunch

Radishes
x 12

Baby carrots
1 bunch

Coriander
1 bunch

 1 drizzle olive oil

👥👥👥👥

🕐

Preparation: 25 minutes
Cooking: 20 minutes

• Chop the **coriander**.
• Peel the **carrots** and **turnips** and trim the radishes. Remove the **cauliflower** stalks and leaves and grate the rest. Spread on a sheet of baking paper and place the other vegetables on top. Cook for 20 minutes in a steamer.
• Serve with the **coriander** and a drizzle of olive oil.

TOMATO, GOATS' CHEESE AND ROSEMARY TART

225 kcal/person

—

Vegetarian

—

Gluten free

Yellow cherry tomatoes
300 g

Fresh goats' cheese
300 g

Eggs
x 4

Rosemary
1 sprig

 **Salt, pepper**

♟♟♟♟

🕑

Preparation: 30 minutes
Cooking: 25 minutes

• Pre-heat the oven to 200°C. Cover the base of a large tart tin with moistened baking paper.
• Mix together the **cheese**, **tomatoes**, cut into pieces, chopped **rosemary** and **eggs**. Season with salt and pepper.
• Pour the mixture into the prepared tin, pressing it down, and bake in the oven for 25 minutes. Serve hot or cold.

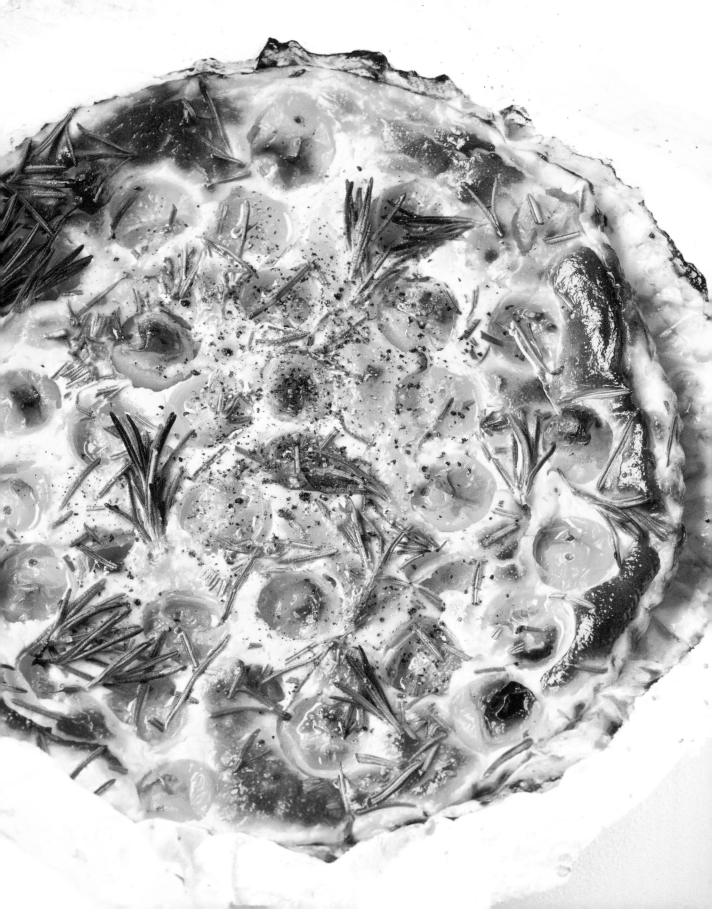

VEGETABLE STEW

31 kcal/person

—

Vegetarian

Golden ball turnips
x 4

Leek
x 1

Carrots
x 4

Sage
1 bunch

 **Salt, pepper**

Preparation: 20 minutes
Cooking: 1 hour

• Wash the **leek** and cut into three lengthways. Peel the **carrots** and **turnips**.
• In a casserole, cook the vegetables with the **sage** in 2 litres of water for 1 hour over very low heat. Season with salt and pepper and serve.

GREEN VEGETABLES IN A RED PEPPER COULIS

117 kcal/person

—

Vegetarian

Red peppers
x 2

Broccoli
200 g

Peas
200 g

Oregano
2 teaspoons

Mange-tout
400 g

Preparation: 10 minutes
Cooking: 25 minutes

• Cook the **mange-tout**, **peas** and the **broccoli**, cut into pieces, for 10 minutes in a steamer.

• In a saucepan, cook the **peppers** in 100 ml water for 15 minutes. Season with salt and pepper and purée with a hand blender.

• Pour the pepper coulis into a serving dish. Top with the vegetables and add the **oregano**.

CLEMENTINE AND PISTACHIO SALAD

118 kcal/person

—

Gluten free

—

Lactose free

Clementines
x 16 (seedless)

Blanched pistachios
2 tablespoons

Tarragon
4 sprigs

Orange flower water
4 tablespoons

Liquid honey
1 tablespoon

Preparation: 30 minutes
Refrigeration:
20 minutes

• Chop the **pistachios**. Mix the **honey** with the **orange flower water**.

• Peel the **clementines** with a very sharp knife and cut into slices.

• Mix all the ingredients together in a salad bowl. Leave to stand for 20 minutes in the refrigerator. Add the chopped **tarragon** and serve.

BLUEBERRY GRATIN

182 kcal/person

—

Gluten free

Blueberries
300 g

Eggs
x 2

Milk
100 ml

Liquid honey
1 tablespoon

Ground almonds
50 g

Preparation: 10 minutes
Cooking: 20 minutes

• Pre-heat the oven to 180°C.
• Beat together the **eggs**, **milk**, **honey** and **ground almonds**.
• Place the **blueberries** in the bottom of 4 small gratin dishes. Pour over the mixture and bake in the oven for 20 minutes. Serve warm or cold.

APRICOT AND ROSEMARY ROLLS

118 kcal/person

—

Lactose free

Apricots
x 8

Rosemary
4 small sprigs

Liquid honey
2 tablespoons

Olive oil
4 tablespoons

Brik pastry
4 sheets

Preparation: 15 minutes
Cooking: 25 minutes

• Pre-heat the oven to 180°C. Stone the **apricots** and cut into pieces.

• Spread out the sheets of **brik pastry** and brush with **olive oil**. Arrange the **apricots** and chopped **rosemary** in the middle of each one. Cover with **honey**. Turn in the sides and roll the pastry sheets up tightly.

• Bake in the oven for 25 minutes. Serve hot.

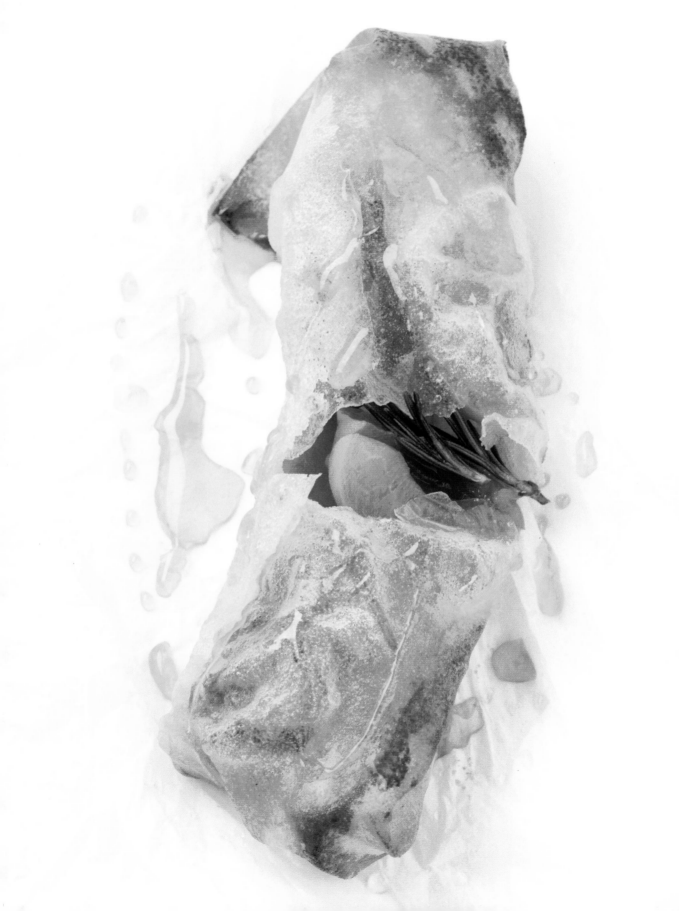

MIXED FRUIT SALAD WITH CHAMPAGNE

161 kcal/person

—

Vegan

—

No added sugar

Strawberries
400 g

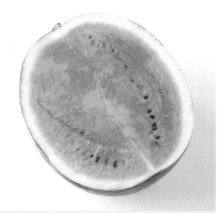

Watermelon
400 g

Blueberries
100 g

Pink Champagne
500 ml (well chilled)

Pink grapefruit
x 1

Preparation: 10 minutes

• De-seed and cut the **watermelon** into small pieces. Place in bowls with the hulled **strawberries**, cut into quarters, and the **blueberries**. Add the strained juice of the **grapefruit**.

• Refrigerate until ready to serve. Pour the pink **Champagne** into the bowls and serve immediately.

CHERRY CLAFOUTIS

133 kcal/person

—

Gluten free

Cherries
x 60

Eggs
x 2

Milk
100 ml

Liquid honey
1 tablespoon

Ground almonds
50 g

Preparation: 20 minutes
Cooking: 25 minutes

• Pre-heat the oven to 180°C
• Beat the **eggs**, **milk**, **honey** and **ground almonds**.
• Stone the **cherries** and place them in a gratin dish. Cover with the egg mixture and bake in the oven for 25 minutes. Serve warm or cold.

COCONUT AND CHOCOLATE BALLS

313 kcal/person

—

Gluten free

Grated coconut
180 g

Chocolate 70% cocoa
6 squares

Eggs
2 whites

Liquid honey
2 tablespoons

Preparation: 15 minutes
Cooking: 5 minutes

• Pre-heat the oven to 210°C.
• Using your fingertips, mix the **egg-whites** with the **honey** and **coconut**. Form into 12 balls and arrange on a baking sheet lined with baking paper, leaving plenty of space in between.
• Insert ½ a square of **chocolate** in the middle of each ball. Bake in the oven for 5 minutes. Allow to cool before serving.

CHERRY SOUP WITH A MINT INFUSION

133 kcal/person

—

Gluten free

—

Lactose free

Cherries
x 32

Mint
1 bunch

Red wine
500 ml

Liquid honey
3 tablespoons

Star anise
x 5

Preparation: 15 minutes
Cooking: 25 minutes
Refrigeration: 1 hour

• Heat the **red wine** with the **honey** and **star anise** for 25 minutes over very low heat. Take off the heat and add the whole bunch of **mint**, reserving a few sprigs for garnish, then leave to cool. Infuse for 1 hour in the refrigerator. Remove the **mint**.

• Stone the **cherries**. Stir into the wine mixture and serve garnished with the reserved **mint** sprigs.

APRICOTS WITH VANILLA AND LEMON

106 kcal/person
—
Vegan

Apricots
x 8

Vanilla
2 pods

Unwaxed lemon
x 1

Sweet white wine
500 ml

Preparation: 10 minutes
Cooking: 45 minutes
Refrigeration: 1 hour

• Pour the **white wine** into a saucepan. Add the **vanilla** (pods split open and scraped) and the zest and juice of the **lemon**. Bring to the boil and reduce to half over low heat.
• Stone the **apricots** and add to the pan. Take off the heat and leave to cool. Infuse in the refrigerator for 1 hour. Serve cold.

LYCHEES AND RASPBERRIES WITH CHAMPAGNE

110 kcal/person

—

Vegan

—

Gluten free

Raspberries
250 g

Lychees
x 20

Mint
8 leaves

Pink Champagne
500 ml (well chilled)

Preparation: 15 minutes

• Peel the **lychees** and cut into pieces. Cut the **raspberries** in half. Slice the **mint** leaves and mix with the fruit. Divide into bowls.
• Refrigerate. Immediately before serving, pour the **pink Champagne** over the fruit.

BAKED APPLES

146 kcal/person
—
Lactose free

Cooking apples
x 4

Prunes
x 8 (stoned)

Hazelnuts
x 20

Liquid honey
4 tablespoons

Flaked almonds
2 tablespoons

Preparation: 10 minutes
Cooking: 20 minutes

• Pre-heat the oven to 180°C.
• Cut 'lids' off the **apples** and scoop out the flesh. Mix the flesh with the **prunes**, cut into small pieces, the chopped **almonds** and **hazelnuts** and the **honey**.
• Stuff the **apples** with the mixture and bake in the oven for 20 minutes. Serve warm.

CHOCOLATE AND RASPBERRY MOUSSE

450 kcal/person

—

Gluten free

Chocolate 70% cocoa
200 g

Eggs
x 6

Raspberries
200 g

Preparation: 20 minutes
Refrigeration: 2 hours

• Separate the **eggs**. Melt the **chocolate** in a bain-marie and mix with the yolks.

• Beat the egg-whites until stiff and fold gently into the melted **chocolate**. Add the **raspberries**, cut into pieces.

• Divide the mousse into 4 ramekins and leave to set for 2 hours in the refrigerator.

354

GRATINATED APRICOTS WITH ALMONDS

64 kcal/person

—

Gluten free

—

Lactose free

Apricots
x 4

Flaked almonds
2 tablespoons

Liquid honey
2 tablespoon

Ground almonds
3 tablespoons

Preparation: 15 minutes
Cooking: 11 minutes

• Pre-heat the oven to 180°C. Stone the **apricots** and cut in half.

• Heat the **honey** with the **ground almonds** and **flaked almonds** for 1 minute, stirring with a spatula.

• Top the **apricot** halves with the honey and almond mixture and bake in the oven for 10 minutes. Serve warm or cold.

PASSION FRUIT WITH CHOCOLATE

105 kcal/person

Passion fruit
x 6

Chocolate 70% cocoa
4 squares

Low-fat cream
4 tablespoons

Preparation: 10 minutes
Cooking: 5 minutes
Refrigeration: 1 hour

• Cut the **passion fruit** in half and scoop out and reserve the pulp. Place the **chocolate** and **cream** in a heatproof bowl and rest over a saucepan of simmering water and melt the **chocolate**, stirring with a spatula. Take off the heat, add the pulp, mix and fill the **passion fruit** with this mixture. Leave for 1 hour in the refrigerator and serve.

LEMON SEMIFREDDO WITH RASPBERRIES

130 kcal/person

—

Gluten free

Lemons
x 4

Raspberries
100 g

Liquid honey
2 tablespoons

Low-fat cream cheese
240 g

Preparation: 15 minutes
Freezing: 1 hour
15 minutes

• Cut 'lids' off the **lemons**. Scoop out the contents with a very sharp knife and reserve the juice.
• Beat the **cream cheese** with the crushed **raspberries**, **honey** and half the reserved **lemon** juice. Spoon into the **lemons** and freeze for 1 hour 15 minutes. Serve semi-frozen.

PEAR AND BLACKBERRY MILLEFEUILLES

91 kcal/person

—

No added sugar

Pears
x 2

Blackberries
100 g

Brik pastry
2 sheets

Vanilla
1 pod

Low-fat cream cheese
120 g

 **1 tablespoon olive oil**

Preparation: 10 minutes
Cooking: 5 minutes

- Pre-heat the oven to 200°C. Brush the sheets of **brik** pastry with olive oil. Bake in the oven for 5 minutes until golden and break into 12 pieces.
- Split the **vanilla** pod and scrape out the seeds.
- Mix the **pears**, cut into pieces, with the crushed blackberries, the **cream cheese** and the vanilla seeds. Arrange spoonfuls of the fruit mixture on plates with pieces of pastry in between.

FRUIT SALAD WITH ROSÉ WINE

222 kcal/person

—

Vegan

—

No added sugar

Cantaloupe melons
x 2

Watermelon
200 g

Blueberries
100 g

Raspberries
200 g

Rosé wine
500 ml

Preparation: 10 minutes
Refrigeration:
15 minutes

• Cut the **cantaloupe melons** in half. Scoop out the flesh, cut into small pieces and mix with the **blueberries**, the halved **raspberries** and the de-seeded and chopped **watermelon**.

• Spoon the fruit into the **melon** halves. Pour over the **rosé wine** and refrigerate for 15 minutes before serving.

NECTARINE GRATIN WITH PINE NUTS

116 kcal/person

—

Gluten free

—

Lactose free

Nectarines
x 4

Pine nuts
3 tablespoons

Ground almonds
3 tablespoons

Orange flower water
3 tablespoons

Liquid honey
2 tablespoons

Preparation: 15 minutes
Cooking: 21 minutes

• Pre-heat the oven to 180°C. Heat the **honey** and the **orange flower water** in a saucepan for 1 minute.

• Stone the **nectarines** and cut into segments. Arrange in an ovenproof dish. Sprinkle with **ground almonds** and **pine nuts**. Pour over the **honey** and orange flower mixture and bake for 20 minutes. Serve warm.

ICED DESSERT WITH MIXED BERRIES

116 kcal/person

—

Gluten free

Mixed berries
250 g

Egg
2 whites

Low-fat cream cheese
120 g

Liquid honey
50 g

Preparation: 25 minutes
Freezing: Overnight

• Mix the crushed **berries** with the **cream cheese**. Beat the **egg-whites** until stiff, then add the warmed **honey**, while beating for a further 1 minute.

• Fold the egg-white mixture into the cream cheese and berry mixture. Transfer to a mould and leave to set overnight in the freezer. Serve in thick slices.

BAKED CHOCOLATE MOUSSE

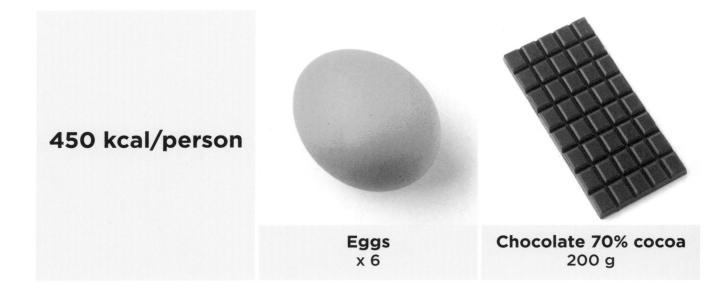

450 kcal/person

Eggs
x 6

Chocolate 70% cocoa
200 g

Cocoa powder
2 tablespoons

Preparation: 15 minutes
Cooking: 9 minutes

• Pre-heat the oven to 200°C. Separate the **eggs**. Melt the **chocolate** in a bain-marie and mix it with the **egg** yolks.

• Beat the whites until stiff and fold gently into the melted **chocolate**.

• Transfer the mousse to ramekins and bake in the oven for 9 minutes. Sprinkle with **cocoa powder** and serve warm.

PEAR GRANITA

65 kcal/person

—

Vegan

—

No added sugar

Pears
x 4 (very ripe)

Basil
8 leaves

Lemon
x 1

Preparation: 15 minutes

• Peel the **pears** and cut into pieces. Mix with the juice of the **lemon**. Refrigerate.

• Just before serving, put half the **pear** in bowls. Purée the remaining **pear** in a blender with the **basil** and 15 ice cubes.

• Top the **pear** pieces with the granita and serve immediately.

CONTENTS

INDEX

An Hachette UK Company
www.hachette.co.uk

First published in Great Britain in 2017 by Hamlyn,
a division of Octopus Publishing Group Ltd
Carmelite House
50 Victoria Embankment
London EC4Y 0DZ
www.octopusbooks.co.uk

First published in France in 2016 by Hachette Livre (Hachette Pratique)
www.hachette-pratique.com

ISBN 978-0-600-63476-8

A CIP catalogue record for this book is available from the British Library

Printed and bound in Spain

10 9 8 7 6 5 4 3 2 1

Director: Catherine Saunier-Talec
Artistic director: Antoine Béon
Editorial director: Céline Le Lamer

Graphic design and layout: Marie-Paule Jaulme
Production: Amélie Latsch

For the UK edition
Group Publishing Director: Denise Bates
Junior Designer: Jack Storey
Designer: Jeremy Tilston
Editor: Natalie Bradley
Translation: Rae Walter, in association with First Edition Translations Ltd, Cambridge, UK
Proofreader: Jane Birch
Indexer: Ingrid Lock
Senior Production Manager: Katherine Hockley